Cultural Landscapes

Editor-in-Chief
Paul Gottfried

Editor
Gabriel R. Ricci

Editorial Board
Harold O.J. Brown
Allan C. Carlson
Jude Doherty
John Gray
Andrew Greeley
Wallance McCaffrey
Jacob Neusner
Robert Nisbet (1913-1996)
Frederick F. Ritsch
Claes G. Ryn
Gerhard Spiegler
Peter J. Stanlis

Assistant Editors
Daniel Jones
Brian Mikulski
Robert Miller
Glenn R. Neufeld
William Patch

Editor

Gabriel R. Ricci

Cultural Landscapes

Religion & Public Life

Volume
35

Transaction Publishers
New Brunswick (U.S.A.) and London (U.K.)

Copyright © 2009 by Transaction Publishers, New Brunswick, New Jersey.

All rights reserved under International and Pan-American Copyright Conventions. No part of this book may be reproduced or transmitted in any form or by any means, electronic or mechanical, including photocopy, recording, or any information storage and retrieval system, without prior permission in writing from the publisher. All inquiries should be addressed to Transaction Publishers, Rutgers—The State University, 35 Berrue Circle, Piscataway, New Jersey 08854-8042. www.transactionpub.com

This book is printed on acid-free paper that meets the American National Standard for Permanence of Paper for Printed Library Materials.

ISSN: 1083-2270
ISBN: 1-4128-0598-8
        978-1-4128-0598-8
Printed in the United States of America

Volumes 1 through 28 were originally published under the title *This World: An Annual of Religion and Public Life.*

Contents

Introduction   vii
   Gabriel R. Ricci

Quest for the Common Good: 1
  A Collaborative Public Theology for a Life-Sustaining Climate
   Jame Schaefer

Three Gorges be Dammed: 23
  The Philosophical Roots of Environmentalism in China
   David L. Kenley

Frontier and Virgin: 39
  The Historical Landscapes of Frederick Jackson
   Turner and Henry Adams
   David S. Brown

Natural Laws: 47
  The Literary and Artistic Roots of American Environmentalism
   Patricia Likos Ricci

What Worlds are Made Of: The Lakota Sense of Place   65
   David Martínez

An Feochàn   73
   Matt Willen

On the Line of the Horizon: Anxiety in de Chirico's   81
  Metaphysical Spaces
   Andreas Philippopoulos-Mihalopoulos

The Use of the Landscape in Heidegger's Philosophy   95
   Gabriel R. Ricci

Contributors   113

Introduction

Gabriel R. Ricci

In his ambition to reconcile Eastern and Western worldviews, Alan Watts used to point out a fundamental mistake that westerners, in particular, neglected to correct. He cautioned, in numerous ways, that the western spiritual traditions obscured the basic insight that we come out of the world, rather than come into the world. To inculcate the latter form of consciousness, Watts argued, is to invite a separation between mind and body, consciousness and world that placed them in opposition to one another. In his promotion of eastern philosophy Watts encouraged a bridging of such cultural divisions that would lead ultimately to a worldview in which we metaphorically conceive our being as a bud that emerges from the energy within a branch; a form of potential energy waiting for the right moment to spring forth. Watts was primarily devoted to a rapprochement between east and west, but his message contains an ecological awareness, one that would find an explicit expression in the ecological poet Gary Snyder, whose work clarified that Nature is not a place to visit; it is home. These insights share the ecological premise that we are vitally linked to interconnected systems, some of which are clearly obvious, others that operate in hidden but life-sustaining ways. Nature, however varied its historical meanings, cannot be conceived as the Other when we are so clearly enveloped by its regulative forces. This perspective is not embraced by everyone. Social constructionists, for example, have revived the nominalism-realism controversy that occupied medieval philosophers to suggest that conceptions of Nature are conventions, changeable linguistic assignments that represent mere mental realities. Such arguments are designed to debunk the misanthropic tree hugger who has deflated the ontological prestige of humanity. Social constructionists do not stop at enumerating the multiple and consequently indecisive meanings of Nature; they boldly claim that Nature is culturally emergent. The coherent social constructionist, of course, is challenged by the fact that humanity is a relatively newcomer to the evolutionary scene; to deny that Nature is the primordial setting for civilization seems disingenuous. There is no debate that we have inherited diverse meanings of Nature, and that they have generated cultural clashes that do not make a biocentric worldview a foregone conclusion, but confusing the historical order between Nature and Culture is an academic artifact without practical merit.

In an appendix to their book *Primitivism and Related Ideas in Antiquity*, Arthur O. Lovejoy and George Boas provide an appendix with an exhaustive list of the many meanings of "Nature." Their enumeration of the multiple meanings of Nature provides instruction on the ethical and normative values of the ancient world, ranging from Aristotle's conception of nature as raw material from which everything is made to the Stoic pantheistic conception of Nature as God and the source of ethical prescriptions. The list also includes the more pejorative views of nature derived from dualistic religions. This inventory is overwhelming and certainly not consistent. However, there is an essential delineation from the ancient world upon which their clarification of Nature rests, the distinction between *physis* and *nomos*, which especially occupied Socrates and the Sophists. On the one hand, *physis* refers to what is primordially provided by the constructive elements of the cosmos and *nomos* refers to social constructs, particularly laws and customs. There is then a fundamental way in which *physis* is both antecedent to culture, society and human history. As such Nature provides a measure or benchmark against which all future constructs might be evaluated. In other words, it makes sense that ancient philosophers, like the Cynics and the Stoics, would look to Nature for normative and ethical guidelines. In this spirit this issue of Religion & Public Life: *Cultural Landscapes*, addresses the physical ways in which we are intimately linked to the land and the intellectual and aesthetic connections human consciousness has with the landscape.

The lead article by Jame Schaeffer, "Quest for the Common Good, A Collaborative Public Theology for a Life-Sustaining Climate," assesses the lightning rod issue of global warming in the context of a public and ecumenical theology based on the common good and classical religious virtues like temperance, humility and prudence. Schaeffer relies on Aquinas for a robust understanding of the common good and latent ecological themes that are consistent with modern environmentalism. While there is the current of stewardship of the Earth running throughout the essay, she looks beyond en ecologically friendly reading of the Scripture to make her case for what she calls a "zone of shared concerns and beliefs" to sustain a coalition of world religions dedicated to the ecological premise she finds in Aquinas' writing. Thus Stoicism, born of the cosmopolitanism of Hellenism and which thrived in the ancient Roman world and early Christianity alike, can also nourish any collaborative effort to address environmental concerns threatening the common good. Schaeffer provides a recent history of the Forum on Religion and Ecology, which is an institutional expression of the urgency to form partnerships to deal with contentious issues like global warming. But there are individual ways to provide solutions that are addressed through international efforts like the Kyoto Protocol: a cultivation of classical religious and philosophical virtues. Schaeffer's "zone of shared concerns and beliefs," then, casts a wide net which is not limited to contemporary activist scholars, the public theology she outlines embraces ancient traditions in which the goals of individual excellence and virtue served the common good.

David Kenley's essay, "Three Gorges be Dammed: The Philosophical Roots of Environmentalism in China," highlights a perennial problem that over the years has effected political fortunes and which has had a dramatic human cost- the flooding of China's great river systems. With the death toll as high as seven million in 1332, two million in 1887 and four million in 1931, it has been virtually impossible for China to exercise its customary reticence about the human loss from the flooding of its longest river, the Hwang Ho or Yellow River. At times like these, China must be reminded of its original flood legend in which the labors of the hero Yu the Great dredged the land and made it safe for agriculture. Today the Chinese have reprised this legendary drama in the Three Gorges Project, which, Kenley notes, has more than technical and financial critics, since it poses obvious environmental hazards and certain death to much of the surrounding vertebrate population.

The emergence of an environmental movement, Kenley argues, is remarkable in light of the negligence that accompanied Mao Zedong's revolution. The rampant environmental degradation resulting from Mao's policies reflects the recalcitrant anthropocentrism of the communist agenda and it is in sharp contrast to the stereotypical image of the traditional spiritual connections represented in Chinese landscape paintings. Kenley reminds us that the new environmental activism in China was embedded in its grand spiritual traditions: Confucianism, Daoism and Buddhism. The controversial Three Gorges Project promises relief to the nation, though it has displaced almost 150,000 people. Hydroelectric power and flood control will be the two most obvious benefits of the 400 square mile reservoir that sits behind a mile and a half dam, but this has not deterred critics like Dai Qing, Kenley reports, because of the long term environmental threats. Though she has been jailed and has had to seek sanctuary in the West, Dai Qing has influenced the judgment of China's environmental protection agency that has levied fines against the construction company for not filing adequate environmental studies.

As China struggles in the infancy of its new environmentalism, it need only look to its intellectual past to enrich ecological consciousness. Like Jame Schaeffer, who enlists classical virtues in the West, Kenley invokes the self-discipline, harmony and even the activism embodied in Confucianism and Daoism. Kenley does not ignore the challenge of Confucianism's anthropocentrism; he finds in the overarching goal of social harmony a logical connection to a more expansive ecological awareness. Likewise Daoism provides spiritual sustenance in the established value of self-discipline, which reverberates with western classical virtues that Jame Schaeffer regards as sympathetic to ecological consciousness.

In 1949, when Aldo Leopold bemoaned the fact that historians have neglected the land and the landscape in the writing of history, he was obviously not aware of how a fellow native Wisconsin had earlier that century defined the writing of history in terms of the idea of the frontier. Frederick Jackson Turner's forays into the wilds of Wisconsin as a young boy would later serve as theoretical backdrop for his career as an historian. In David Brown's essay "Frontier and Virgin: The Historical Landscapes of Frederick Jackson Turner and Henry Adams," he examines the early life of the American Historical Society through the influential work of Frederick Jackson Turner and Henry Adams. Though these two historians would adopt contrasting paradigms, they would in the end agree on the threat of decline to the old American way of life. While Turner used the archetype of the frontier to define and promote what he perceived as unique American character, Adams' attachment was to the Gothic European world that gave birth to the model of the Virgin as embodied in Mont Saint Michel and Chartres cathedral. Adams identified with the clustered narratives nestled in the tympanum and transepts of Chartres cathedral, a story of a benign paternalistic world in which cosmological hierarchies opposed democratic sensibilities. In his famous argument for the medieval bases of Western thought, E.R. Curtius regarded Adams' turn to Europe as a pilgrimage of someone who had set out to find his long lost mother. Led by the instinct of his race, Curtius surmised, Adams' vision of America was forged by Dante as well as Puritanism and William Penn.

According to Brown, however, these contrasting models reflected a larger debate at the time: whether or not history was a science or art. Turner, for example, invoked Darwin in his writing, an obvious result of his infatuation with the wilderness. On the other hand, Adams' historical sensibility was shaped by encroaching industrialization and the threat of collapsing social divisions. In the end both historians would overcome their differences in the shared preoccupation with decline, a decline that manifested itself in the new waves of immigration. Both Turner and Adams, Brown reports, were quite vocal in their opposition to the non-Northern European immigrant. Their mutual vision consisted of a cultural and racial homogeneity that Italians, Poles, Slovaks and Jews threatened to upset, since they did not adequately appreciate the farming model upon which America's greatness and uniqueness rested. Decrying the resistance to assimilate to the established process that Turner identified in terms of the agrarian model, Brown suggests, was more than a gentleman's polite expression of racism; Turner was really heralding a threat to the social organism of America.

An earlier movement in the United States exemplified what Leopold would later call the "ecological conscience." Patricia Likos Ricci's essay, "Natural Laws: The Literary and Artistic Roots of American Environmentalism," traces the connection between the Wilderness Act of 1964 and the Endangered Species Act of 1973, which legally recognized the natural rights of ecosystems and their inhabitants, to the environmental ethos that emerged during the first half of the nineteenth century. Why New York State emerged as the locus of legal innovation is explained in part by the discovery of mastodon fossils in the Hudson River Valley that offered conclusive proof of the extinction of species. The new understanding of irreversible natural processes made the flora and fauna of America precious to the first generations to live under the shadow of extinction.

As Likos Ricci describes, artists-naturalists, landscape painters, novelists and poets urged their contemporaries to safeguard portions of the wilderness which was then being consumed in the name of progress. They fought an up-hill battle against the staunch individualism and democratization of property that pit the interests of the rising middle-class against the survival of the old-growth forests of the Northeast. Washington Irving, James Fennimore Cooper, William Cullen Bryant and Thomas Cole laid the foundations for environmental preservation by extolling the wilderness as the unique and distinguishing feature of the United States on whom Providence had bestowed the stewardship of the primordial landscape. Cooper and Cole in particular were devout Christians who believed the wanton disregard for God's creatures was sinful. They condemned the notion that other life forms were merely property, arguing that they were entitled to life under the same principle of natural law on which the United States was founded, and introduced the idea that the preservation of wilderness for the benefit of future generation was a patriotic duty. Cole went further, warning in his pictorial narrative, *The Course of Empire,* that unchecked consumption and expansionism could bring about the downfall of a civilization.

In "What Worlds are Made Of: The Lakota Sense of Place," David Martinez explains how attachment to the land is realized through mythic tales that link a people to the cosmogonic past. On the basis of Rudolf Otto's insights in *Das Heilige*, Mircea Eliade described these sorts of perceptions as a religious experience in which the world is experienced as non-homogenous with the sacred spontaneously erupting into the profane. Traditional cultures are informed by the consecration of place through its creation mythology. Martinez's essay provides insight into the Lakota sense of place by way of storytelling and analysis.

There are real legal concerns that occupy the Lakota Nation, but Martinez focuses on the manner in which homeland is not restricted to mere space identifiable on a map, but which occupies a spiritual sphere. The map upon which a homeland is located is a mental and symbolic map that expands into cosmic domains and stretches back to a mythical past. (Such appeals to a mythical past are generally associated with archaic and so-called primitive cultures, but the power of these connections was not lost on the ancient Greeks and Romans who were notorious for exalting mythical ancestry that bestowed political status and military prowess.) Obviously, then, any claims to land from this perspective would challenge any conventional legal system. Such a drama was played out in Werner Herzog's 1984 film, *Where the Green Ants Dream*, in which Aboriginal claims to sacred space are not readily understood by modern western legal standards. The film depicts the cultural clash between a society whose claims to land are entrenched in the labor theory of value and claims to a homeland that are determined by attention and care to locations where the dreaming of the green ants preserves cosmic order. To neglect the care of such sacred spaces is to endanger the entire universe. Theirs is not a legal title to land but a valid claim to destiny, as Martinez argues on behalf of the Lakota. The real difference in these cultural discrepancies is between labor that exploits the land and care that makes a place out of mere space.

Matt Willen's poetic insights into the traditional Irish Air demonstrate the vital connections between the human spirit and the natural world. His personal account in "An Feochán" explores the spiritual and transformative powers of a form of music that transcends self-expression and reaches into the history of a people and place.

Willen relies on the sensibility of Wordsworth and Rilke to convey the spiritual and religious transcendence embodied in the Air, an experience in which the internal depths of the fiddler are creatively conflated with the environment in which the music is played. Willen uses Rilke's expression "holy departure" to communicate this improvisational quality of the Air. Technically this quality is enhanced by the rubato style of playing that liberally restructures the length of notes ascending like a current up and down the octave, but the immediate environment always guarantees the fleeting nature of the Air. This means that there can be no final transcription to rely on in an Air; in the end the confluence of the fiddler's spirit and his environs determines how the music is played. The spontaneity of the Air that is derived from being wrapped in history and being attuned to place musically verifies Alan Watts' intuition that we come out of the world, we do not come in to the world.

Andreas Philippopoulos-Mihalopoulos' essay "On the Line of the Horizon, Anxiety in de Chirico's Metaphysical Spaces" provides the reader with psychological and existential insights into the disorienting paintings of de Chirico, one of the founders of the Metaphysical School of painting in the early twentieth century. Informed by visions of a bygone classical era, de Chirico managed to combine incompatible spatial systems and ambiguous horizons into one coherent image. What Philippopoulos-Mihalopoulos defines as a palimpsestic spatiotemporal treatment of the landscape is framed within Husserlian insights and described against the backdrop of the romantic conception of *Stimmung* or the interior mood of aesthetic intuition.

De Chirico's early metaphysical paintings are linked to his reading of Nietzsche's *The Birth of Tragedy*. Behind Nietzsche's explanation of the antagonistic forces in the evolution of aesthetic forms is the goal of exploring the intuition that everyday reality is an illusion and merely conceals another totally different reality. De Chirico's ambition was to represent this intuition; he intended his painting of the quotidian to reveal an obscured metaphysical realm. This dream reality is depicted in de Chirico's series of Ariadne paintings, one of which is illustrated here. De Chirico's disquieting paintings would inspire the irreverence of Dadism, but de Chirico's *pitturra metafisica* were intended as aesthetic provocations that would mediate the reality of dreams and their application to real life. Dadism responded to the hypocrisy of the military machine embraced by Christian culture during World War I.

Philippopoulos-Mihalopoulos explains how Kierkegaard's philosophical insights can orient us to de Chirico's work but to understand the sense of prehistory incorporated into his work, specifically his horizons, Heidegger's temporal ontology can provide a literary key. By a sense of prehistory de Chirico meant the echoing of origins and a concerted turn to the past. This turning included more that the use of classical imagery, it was a spatiotemporal fusion of the kind found in Heidegger's rendering of human existence or *Dasein*. *Dasein*, like de Chirico's horizons, constitutes an ecstatical unity or more precisely a temporality that is defined in terms of a present "in-order-to", a past of "what-has-been" and a future "for-the-sake-of-which". Heidegger consolidates this existential state in the term *Sorge* or Care and he intended a literary version of the pictorial window onto the infinite that is a recurring motif in de Chirico's work.

Heidegger's philosophy may well present a literary analogue to de Chirico's metaphysical paintings, but independently Heidegger's ontological musings are illustrated by a habitual reference to the landscape, a landscape that he personally encountered. In the final essay I explore the philosophical landscape in Heidegger's work beginning with the early manifestations of the *Lichtung* or forest clearing in *Being and Time* to its later incarnations in his essay *Zur Erörterung der Gelassenheit*. There is a long list of metaphors from the landscape that underpin Heidegger's fundamental ontology and which essentially make up the temporal environment in which *Dasein* dwells. The umbrella concept of Care stipulates that human existence is attached to being-in-a-world that is immediately an object of concern and solicitude.

I basically extract an environmental philosophy from Heidegger's body of work which corresponds to some of the tenets of ecofeminism, an environmental worldview that critiques the hegemony of Enlightenment rationalism and its accompanying invasive technological will. Heidegger was occupied with a critique of the technological invasiveness of culture in the thirties and forties and took pains to single out the burgeoning consumerism of the West, particularly in the United States. After the Second World War this sort of criticism could only have been construed as sour grapes but the unmistakable sensitivity to the environment can not be ignored. Form his earliest philosophical writings; Heidegger actively challenged the Cartesian legacy that proof of existence is a methodological obligation. Such intellectual preoccupations ignore the world into which we are thrown and the emotional awareness that predisposes us to vital attachments to the environment.

Quest for the Common Good: A Collaborative Public Theology for a Life-Sustaining Climate

Jame Schaefer

Over-consumption of natural goods in industrially developed countries. Accumulation of hazardous and household wastes. Widespread water and air pollution. Acceleration of the rate of species extinction and loss of biodiversity. Degradation and destruction of wetlands, prairies, and other ecological systems. Threats to the integrity of the biosphere. Unjust adverse effects on the most vulnerable humans. Global warming.

Increasing awareness of these and other indicators of environmental abuse have been prompting scholars of the world's religions to examine their traditions and identify meaningful ways of responding. Recent scientific findings that our planet's temperature has risen due to emissions of carbonic compounds from industrial processes, electricity generation, and road vehicles have prompted religious communities to pressure decision-makers to restrict the emitting of these compounds. The United States' refusal to join other nations in reducing emissions by specified dates has prompted increasing interest among religions to collaborate in launching a public effort to address the causes of global warming at all levels of social, economic, and political life. Key to this effort is a clearly articulated public theology that will provide a shared rationale for initiating and sustaining action.

This essay focuses primarily on collaborative efforts by religions to address global warming that threatens a good that is common to all living beings—a life-sustaining planet. I begin by exploring the theological idea of the common good as reflected upon traditionally from the perspective of the human good of all and extended more recently to encompass the common good of the biosphere. Subsequently overviewed are efforts by representative leaders and scholars of world religions to reflect on their various traditions and by religious groups to alert believers to their personal responsibilities and opportunities for bringing shared concerns into the political arena. Moving to global warming as a key issue, I review divergent scientific views pertaining to global warming, the theological perspectives from which religious groups are responding to scientific findings, and the cooperation of some major Christian and Jewish organizations to address this issue under the umbrella of an ecumenical partnership. I conclude by delving more deeply into the religious traditions of the partners and identifying some beliefs that could frame a constructive public theology upon which the partnership can rely to guide its efforts.

The Common Good

Traditionally, reflections on the common good have focused on the human community with particular concern for poor and disadvantaged people who are unable to achieve goods they need to sustain their lives. David Hollenbach's overview of that perspective in Christian ethical discourse is particularly instructive,[1] while a plethora of scholars have explored the notion of the common good historically to the present from various concerns in essays[2] and monographs.[3] Defined and promoted vigorously by the Catholic tradition,[4] the concept of the common good stresses the need to have workable social systems, institutions, and environments on which humans depend to benefit all people, not only those who enjoy the wealth and power through which to secure their well-being. Some examples of particular common goods or parts thereof include a just political and legal system, a thriving educational system open to all, a flourishing economic system in which people can find employment and provide for their needs, an accessible and affordable public health care system, an effective system of public safety and security, peace among the nations of the world, and a healthy natural environment. The common good approach to ethics assumes a society of individuals whose own good is inextricably linked to the good of the community and whose members are bound by a pursuit of common values and goals. This approach also assumes that the cooperation of many is often required to pursue a common good. A good counts as common only to the extent that it is accessible to *all* people.

Religious and secular calls for a commitment to the common good tempers concern for the rights of individuals, and most fundamental social problems seem to grow out of a widespread pursuit of individual interests to the exclusion of concern for others. Recent appeals to the common good have surfaced in discussions of the social responsibilities of businesses, genetic manipulation, lack of investment in education, problems of crime and poverty, media reporting, access to political power, and environmental degradation.

William C. French extends traditional thinking about the common good to encompass more than humans. Insisting that there are many resources upon which to draw for developing a biospheric common good, he points specifically to three: the Noachic covenant in the Book of Genesis; the Stoic conception of the universal community; and, Thomas Aquinas's teachings on creation.[5] French perceptively finds permeating Aquinas's creation theology a "cosmological-ecological principle" wherein each diverse constituent exists for the sake of the whole universe. This dominant organizing principle provides a promising response to our current ecological morass, French argues, by requiring humans, individually and collectively, to consider the good of all beings when functioning in political, economic, and social life.[6]

More can be said about Aquinas's teachings on the common good, as French encourages. Appropriating the Aristotelian understanding of the world when reflecting on the Christian faith, Aquinas taught that God created many diverse creatures to interact with one another in ways that assure their good and the good of the whole universe.[7] Each constituent has an essential role to play in the whole, he contended, and all creatures are required for the proper functioning of the whole—contingent and non-contingent, corporeal and incorporeal, corruptible and incorruptible.[8] He maintained that there is a natural inclination of each part toward the common good of the whole that God instilled in each creature,[9] with each creature inclined toward the common good in ways that are conducive to their type of existence.[10] For Aquinas, following Aristotle, the unique character of human existence is our ability to think rationally and make informed decisions.

While all entities that constitute the universe are inclined toward the common good of the whole, Aquinas taught, the more perfect a thing is in its power and the higher it is on the scale of goodness, the more it has an appetite for the broader common good and the more it seeks to become involved in doing good for beings far removed from itself.[11] Imperfect beings tend only to the good that is appropriate to the individual, while the more perfect a thing is, the more widely it diffuses its goodness.[12] From this perspective, if humans are more endowed with rational capacities that other beings do not have, humans should become involved in discerning and acting on behalf of the good for others and their shared common good.

Aquinas maintained that all constituents benefit from being moved toward the common good of the whole. For example, the ordering of all parts to the good of the whole is what a leader of an army does when intending the common good of soldiers.[13] All parts benefit from the ordering of parts to one another that enables them to function appropriately to bring about the good of the whole. Furthermore, the order that binds things together makes whatever belongs to any one part belong somehow to all.[14]

For Aquinas, all creatures are intended by God to cooperate for the good of the whole. In the operations of unintelligible beings, there is almost always harmony and usefulness among them because they are directed toward their ends, their purposes for existing, by God.[15] God also intends harmony and cooperation to prevail among all diverse beings that constitute the universe.[16] As Legrand observed from Aquinas' teachings, no part of creation or type of creature is excluded from God's intentions that all cooperate, combine, or harmonize within the order of the universe to achieve their common good.[17]

The collaboration of all constituents of the universe to achieve their common good is the greatest created good, according to Aquinas. He described the ordered activity of beings that bring about their unity as marvelous,[18] and he used an array of other superlatives to laud the interactions of creatures that bring about their common good as intended by God. For Aquinas, the interaction of creatures is nothing less than the greatest good, the highest perfection of the created world, and its most beautiful attribute.[19] As Wright described Aquinas's understanding about the universe, it is "God's masterpiece" and its excellence is found in the ordered harmony of its parts.[20]

In light of the evidence of adverse effects on the natural environment enumerated at the beginning of this article, especially scientific evidence that Earth's temperature has risen, humans have not been thinking rationally, making informed decisions, and functioning cooperatively with other constituents of Earth. Awareness of this ongoing degradation of the natural environment and predictions of increasing threats to the ecological systems within which humans function have prompted leaders of the world religions to appeal to their respective followers to change attitudes and actions that are precipitating the global warming threat to a life-sustaining planet. Scholars of the world religions have been perusing their sources for helpful ways in which believers can think and act more responsibly to mitigate human-caused changes in Earth's climate. And, groups of believers who follow the various traditions have been organizing to advocate ameliorative and preventive actions at all levels of social, political, and economic life. To these efforts we now turn.

Religious Advocacy and Scholarly Efforts for a Common Good

Leaders of the world's religions individually, collectively, and in collaboration with scientists have issued numerous statements calling their faith-filled followers to awareness of local to global threats to the natural environment and to action. An early initiative by leaders of Buddhism, Christianity, Hinduism, Judaism, and Islam was prompted by the World Wildlife Fund on the twenty-fifth anniversary of its founding who invited them to stipulate how their respective faiths guide them in caring for the environment. Representatives of the five religions met in Assisi, Italy in September 1987 and issued declarations to their followers. Three more faiths—Baha'i, Jainism, and Sikhism—subsequently issued their declarations.[21] When thirty-two outstanding scientists wrote "An Open Letter to the Religious Community" in January 1990 encouraging "a spirit of common cause and joint action to help preserve the Earth," two hundred and seventy-one well-known spiritual leaders–patriarchs, lamas, chief rabbis, cardinals, mullahs, archbishops, and professors of theology—from eighty-three countries signed their names to the scientists' document in solidarity with their mutual concern about the natural environment.[22]

Among later efforts initiated by religious leaders without any prompting by environmentalists was the first statement issued in 1990 by a pope of the Roman Catholic Church that was dedicated exclusively to addressing the ecological crisis as a common moral responsibility.[23] In 1997, the spiritual leader of Orthodox Christians, Patriarch Bartholomew I of Constantinople, denounced environmental abuse as a "sin against God, humanity, and nature," and followed up his declaration with a number of actions for which he has been dubbed the "Green Patriarch."[24] He and Pope John Paul II of the Roman Catholic Church co-signed the Venice Declaration on the Environment in 2002 in which they invited reflection on six ethical goals and seeking solutions to environmental problems in the interests of future generations.[25] Many statements have been issued by the National Council of Churches of Christ, including the most recent in February 2005,[26] and by bishops of the Roman Catholic Church in response to the Pope's 1990 World Day of Peace Message.[27] Jewish leaders have responded to the environmental crisis through various efforts sponsored by the Coalition on the Environment and Jewish Life.[28] The Islamic Foundation for Ecology and Environmental Sciences has articulated the Islamic position on environmental matters while engaging in research, teaching, and conducting experiments on land use, organic farming, and the development of alternative technologies.[29] Many denominations of Christian churches have established Justice, Peace, and Integrity of Creation ministries to pursue the interconnection of these issues theologically and practically,[30] while other religious groups have organized study and advocacy programs.[31]

Collaborative efforts have marshaled energy and resources to address environmental concerns including global warming. An effort initiated by four major religious organizations in the United States—the Coalition on the Environment and Jewish Life, the Evangelical Environmental Network, the National Council of Churches of Christ, and the United States Conference of Catholic Bishops—lead to the formation of the National Religious Partnership for the Environment in 1993 whose shared mission is "to care for God's creation throughout religious life, once and for all."[32] Other collaborations include the Parliament of World Religions which was held in Chicago in 1993, attended by some eight thousand people from all over the globe, and issued a Global Ethics of Cooperation of Religions on Human and Environmental Issues statement. Another international effort was the Global Forum of Spiritual and Parliamentary Leaders which has held conferences in Oxford (1988), Moscow (1990), Rio (1992), and Kyoto (1993), involving religious leaders as well as diplomats and heads of nations in addressing several issues including the environmental crisis. Since 1995, the Alliance of Religions and Conservation has been convening conferences in England and publishing books on this topic.[33]

Scholarly endeavors to address environmental concerns have been prolific in the past three decades as evidenced by the plethora of articles in academic journals, essays in anthologies, and books that have been published.[34] A major initiative to engage scholars of the world religions in critically examining their traditions for fruitful ways of responding to environmental degradation was conducted through a series of conferences from 1996 to 1998 at Harvard University. These conferences yielded ten volumes published from 1997 to 2004 with each focusing on a world religion (Buddhism, Christianity, Confucianism, Daoism, Hinduism, Indigenous Traditions, Jainism, Judaism, Islam, and Shinto) in relation to ecology.[35] The Forum on Religion and Ecology was organized subsequently to help develop "religion and ecology as an academic area of study and research in universities, colleges, seminaries, and other religiously affiliated institutions."[36] Recognizing that religions need to be in dialogue with other disciplines (e.g., science, ethics, economics, education, public policy, and gender) in order to seek comprehensive solutions to both global and local environmental problems, the Forum encourages innovative research that interfaces religion and ecology, develops and promotes educational programs, and fosters the intersection of religious traditions with other disciplines engaged in environmental studies.[37]

The Contentious Phenomenon of Global Warming

One scientific finding that is riveting the attention of religious organizations, environmental groups, and scholars is the increase of 0.8 percent in the average temperature on Earth. Scientists attribute this phenomenon to several gases emitted into the atmosphere where they remain in its upper regions and trap the planet's heat, a condition dubbed as "the greenhouse effect." The most prevalent of the greenhouse gases is carbon dioxide, a molecule that is emitted naturally by humans and other animals but the bulk of which comes from burning fossil fuels that are used in automobiles, industrial production, and the generation of energy. Scientific alerts to these threats have been ongoing, with the most recent having been issued by the national science academies of Brazil, Canada, China, France, Germany, India, Italy, Japan, Russia, the United Kingdom, and the United States in June 2005.[38]

Scientific predictions about future adverse effects if this warming trend continues include danger to human health, dislocation of populations, increasing intensity of extreme weather events such as storms, floods and droughts, and damage to fragile ecological systems. Some of these effects are likely if the predictions issued by the United Nation's Intergovernmental Panel on Climate Change predictions hold that temperatures will rise 1.4°C (2.5°F) to 5.8°C (10.4 °F) by 2100.[39] Predicting the future is wrought with uncertainties,[40] but the compelling evidence from honed modeling technologies has prompted a number of initiatives to mitigate anticipated effects. Among these are recommendations to industrialized and developing nations issued in January 2005 by the International Climate Change Taskforce to prevent the average global temperature from rising more than 2° C above the pre-industrial level.[41]

Another recent initiative to mitigate global warming was made by mayors of cities around the world during the celebration of the 2005 United Nations World Environment Day in San Francisco, California. The mayors signed on June 5 the Urban Environmental Accords, an international treaty aimed at taking actions that will limit the emission of greenhouse gases in their municipalities.[42] Also announced during this time was an executive order issued by California Governor Arnold Schwarzenegger to State officials to reduce emission of greenhouse gases to 2000 levels by 2010, 1990 levels by 2020, and 80 percent below 1990 levels by 2050. The Secretary of California's Environmental Protection Agency is charged with overseeing efforts to meet these goals and with reporting progress in January 2006 as well as every six months thereafter.[43]

A major international effort to lessen the predicted effects of global warming is the Kyoto Protocol to the United Nations Framework Convention on Climate Change. Negotiated in Japan in December 1997, opened for signature by nations on March 16, 1998, and effective on February 16, 2005 following ratification by Russia, the Protocol requires industrialized nations to cut greenhouse gas emissions by an average of five percent below 1990 levels.[44] Some current estimates indicate that, even if successfully and completely implemented, the Protocol is anticipated to reduce the average global temperature by somewhere between 0.02° C and 0.28° C by the year 2050.[45] Unfortunately, the world's largest emitter of greenhouse gases, the United States of America, has not ratified the Protocol, primarily due to an estimated loss of jobs and higher energy prices. United States President George W. Bush underscored this rationale at the July 2005 meeting of the "Group of Eight" major economic nations held in Scotland, prompting British Prime Minister Tony Blair, who hosted the gathering, to announce the initiation of a "new Dialogue" between the G8 and emerging economies of the world "to slow down and then, in time, to reverse the rise of harmful greenhouse gas emissions."[46] Dialogue is scheduled to begin in November 2005 in Great Britain. In the meantime, the other seven of the G8 nations who have signed the Kyoto Protocol will continue their work toward its goal while the United States focuses on providing improved access to cleaner and more secure energy resources with the aim of reducing "the growth of greenhouse gas emissions associated with long-term climate change."[47]

Aware of the dire predictions amidst some dissenting opinions about the future dangers of global warming, religious leaders and organizations have rallied to study the scientific findings and political responses to these findings. Particularly problematic for religious groups in the United States is the federal government's refusal to sign the Kyoto Protocol and to make concerted efforts to restrict emissions of greenhouse gases. The National Religious Partnership for the Environment and its individual partners have issued at least seventy-four documents[48] calling followers of their various Christian and Jewish denominations to become aware of the issues pertaining to global warming and their moral responsibilities as prescribed by their respective religious faiths.[49] Recognizing the many benefits of working closely together on this shared concern, the Partnership is launching a fully collaborative effort to address global warming. This effort will require identifying meaningful shared principles in a public theology that can be used to motivate staff, the partners, and their constituents.

A Public Theology for a Common Good—A Life-Sustaining Climate

Dismissing the contention that growing religious pluralism makes a shared understanding of the common good increasingly improbable, Hollenbach argues convincingly from empirical evidence[50] that religious leaders and communities have made contributions to fostering the idea and reality of the common good into public life.[51] Furthermore, he insists that religious communities are "uniquely positioned to make contributions to sustaining a vision of the common good and empowering their members to participate" in pursuing it in the public arena.[52] Religious communities can make these contributions because they can tap into the inspiring sources of their traditions and, as Hollenbach insists persuasively, can provide the motivation for becoming politically active in order to realize the values engendered in and through their religious beliefs.[53]

A life-sustaining climate is indeed a common good that the constituents of the National Religious Partnership for the Environment share on behalf of followers of their various Christian and Jewish denominations. They also share a foundational belief that God is the ultimate creator of the universe, the world would not be if it were not for God's willing and sustaining its existence, and humans are responsible to God to care for God's creation. This shared faith provides the basis for their ecumenical collaboration to address the phenomenon of global warming and to take action to mitigate its adverse effects. These basic foundations for responding to the global warming phenomenon qualify under what theologians Michael J. and Kenneth R. Himes describe as "a zone of shared concerns and beliefs" among those who "desire to move religious belief away from a narrow concern with personal life" and into the pubic sphere[54] to address moral issues. By entering the public arena to address this urgent moral issue of global warming has an additional benefit of contributing to the well-being of the global society by helping to shape public life.[55]

Vital to the task of initiating a major collaborative effort to address global warming in the public arena is paying sufficient attention to the theological foundations for action. The Himeses stress the need "to make explicit the theological component of social ethics so believers can understand and test the coherence of their religious beliefs with their public policy decisions."[56] Crucial to undertaking the articulation of a public theology to address global warming is delving as deeply as possible into the religious traditions of the partners to provide what they identify as "an underlying set of ideas" with sufficient depth and consistency[57] to motivate the partners, their constituents, and their staff to undertake and sustain a major collaborative effort to address global warming in the public arena. Depth in theological foundations for this task is also vital to motivate the followers of the religious traditions represented by the National Religious Partnership for the Environment to become involved at all levels of social, economic, and political life.

Finding a common theological ground for religions to address global warming is key, as theologian Thomas Hughson advocates in another context.[58] In his appeal for collaboration among religionists, Hughson stresses the need for deliberation and reflection on the "normative meaning and empirical potential" of religion in the public arena to seek the common good.[59]

An effective collaborative effort must begin with recognizing shared theological principles. Many pertaining to energy and global warming have appeared in seventy-four documents in various formats that have been issued by the Partnership, by its constituents individually, and by two partners (the National Council of Churches of Christ and the Coalition on the Environment and Jewish Life) in cooperation with one another as the Interfaith Climate and Energy Campaign. A variety of scriptural references, theological principles, and ethical norms have been relied upon to prompt reflection and promote action. Several cohere as core principles that could serve as a basis for developing a religiously motivated political campaign and preparing the partners' constituents for collective action. Some principles diverge or are emphasized in unique ways by a partner and can be used to motivate its individual constituents. Other principles that are promising for addressing global warming have been mentioned, but they need full development in order to press the case for preventing or mitigating the effects of global warming.

Shared Religious Beliefs

Responsibility to care for Earth prevails as the major principle shared by the four partners. That humans are stewards of God's creation who are responsible to God for the care of Earth resounds in thirty of the seventy-four documents surveyed.[60] Nine of these and one additional document underscore the belief that Earth belongs to God.[61] When launching a national global warming campaign, the meaning of stewardship and the role of steward need to be clearly defined, and responsibility to God for how they care for Earth underscored. Especially important is recognizing that stewards need to *manage themselves* in light of the adverse effects caused humans have and continue to cause to the life-supporting processes of Earth.[62] Among the significant prohibitions that can contribute to this definition is the principle of *Bal Tashchit*—do not destroy or waste—proffered by the Coalition on Environment and Jewish Life.[63] Stewards are not destructive of God's good creation nor do they waste it by actions that cause global warming, as several other surveyed documents indicate explicitly.[64] I return in the third section of this part to another idea to retrieve for determining *how* to care for Earth.

Concern for the poor and powerless reigns as a close second principle among the partners, as expressed variously in twenty-six of the documents surveyed.[65] As the references to biblical texts demonstrate, the partners draw from the Hebrew prophets who admonished the ancient Israelites for their social injustices and called them to care for the poor, the widows, and the orphans. Showing how poor and powerless people are being affected by global warming and may be affected in the future is vital to the national campaign launched by the Partnership.[66]

One aspect of social justice is the partners' agreement that God gifts to all people the diverse animate and inanimate goods of Earth. Sixteen documents underscore this belief.[67] Among the issues that a national campaign needs to address is overuse of these goods by some people to the detriment of others. The overuse by industrially developed countries of non-renewable energy sources that emit greenhouse gases is a case in point, especially when renewable energy sources are barely tapped. Developing nations not only suffer from or are threatened by global warming due to the accumulation of these gases. They also suffer from the unavailability of renewable energy technologies that could facilitate the health and well being of their people.

Another aspect of social justice shared by the four partners is concern for future humans, a principle that is stressed in thirteen documents.[68] If some of the dire predictions of climate change occur, future humans will be the "new poor" who are adversely affected and deprived of the goods of Earth and whose access to a life-sustaining planet is being threatened by global warming. Since the documents deal primarily with justice to humans, the partners may consider extending the notion of justice to the non-human poor—other species, their habitats, and ecological systems that may be affected adversely by global warming. They are constituents of God's creation, they have basic needs to be met for their survival and functioning, and their survival is intricately linked to human health and well-being.

While the love of neighbor may be implicit in all partners' commitments to social justice, this call was expressed explicitly in six documents issued by the Evangelical Environmental Network and two constituents of the National Council of Churches of Christ.[69] Believing that God calls humans to a loving relationship with one another may be a powerful motivating principle for a national campaign, but a clear endorsement of this principle of faith by the four partners is needed. Of course, one's neighbor must be identified as near and far, now and into the future.

Finally, the goodness of God's Earth is a shared valuation by the four partners as indicated explicitly in eight key documents.[70] The intrinsic value of Earth needs to be balanced, however, by the instrumental valuing in the interests of humans to justify the human use of other planetary constituents to provide the necessities of life. Some of the partners recognize that the superlative valuation is for the entirety of creation and not exclusively for humanity,[71] which in turn can aid a national campaign dealing with the worldwide ramifications of global warming.

Unique and Promising Principles

Individual partners and constituents of the National Council of Churches of Christ have based their advocacy positions on principles that are unique to their particular ways of expressing their religious faith. Some of these principles may also be retrievable from other partners' theological traditions but are not expressed in the documents surveyed. Where they diverge from the other partners, the principles ascribed to by a partner can be explored and reflected upon for development and action from within its membership when launching a national global warming campaign. The more the partner calls upon the shared faith of its members to stimulate their thinking and motivate their responsible actions, the more effective a campaign may be.

One principle articulated by two partners is the faith perspective that the condition of human sinfulness affects the entirety of creation. This view is noted in six documents issued by the Evangelical Environmental Network, the National Council of Churches of Christ, and one of the Council's constituents, the Reformed Church of America.[72] In order to avoid thinking that the "fallen" nature of humanity is responsible for the adversities caused by global warming, individual and collective human acts that precipitate climate change must be presented as moral choices that humans can and should avoid.

The desire to achieve the common good is expressed in five documents by two partners, the Coalition on Environment and Jewish Life and the United States Conference of Catholic Bishops.[73] Articulating the common good as explicitly as possible and the extent to which individual goods are to be sacrificed for the communal good is essential. Clearly, the good of all humans and other entities upon which humans depend for their material sustenance is a life-sustaining planet. As scientific reports indicate, global warming threatens life on Earth. Poor people and nations are least able to protect themselves from the adverse effects, and establishing "solidarity" with them is a key commitment underscored by the Conference of Catholic bishops in several documents.[74]

While avoiding wastefulness when using the sources of Earth may be implicit in the four partners' call to stewardship, the Coalition on Environment and Jewish Life articulated this principle explicitly as *Bal Tashchit*, while the Presbyterian Church USA expressed the need to examine patterns of consumption.[75] Identifying wasteful practices that are contributing to global warming is essential to a national campaign, and vital to this task is pointing to the specific levels of socioeconomic life at which wasteful practices can be avoided and moderate use practices can be implemented. The partners can examine their traditions for insightful and inspiring sources that promote moderate living and discourage wastefulness. Among them is the virtue of temperance which links closely with the virtue of justice that the four partners embrace. In addition to promoting these virtues as individual characteristics to develop, translating these two virtues into collective action and bringing them into the public arena where necessary is vital to a national global warming campaign.

Two other virtues that have significance for a national campaign are humility and prudence. They were mentioned twice in literature issued by the Interfaith Climate and Energy Campaign, while prudence was emphasized by the Conference of Catholic Bishops.[76] In Thomistic theology, which is embraced especially by the Catholic tradition, humility is a sub-virtue of temperance,[77] while the virtue of prudence is the primary virtue that informs the other moral virtues.[78] The virtue of prudence requires considerable development by the partners, as recommended in the next section of this paper, not only to underscore the distinguishing characteristics of the human species but also the responsibility incumbent upon humans to make informed decisions and act on them. Key to incorporating the virtue of humility into a national campaign is recognizing the human place within the creation as intricately interconnected with other species, the air, the land, and the water and as radically dependent upon them for human well-being. The Presbyterian Church USA stressed the latter point in one document when reflecting on the life-supporting processes of Earth.[79] An absence of humility can be seen in the havoc that humans have caused to themselves, other species, and ecological systems as well as in the abuse of technological power through which human operators have degraded ecological systems and the biosphere of Earth.

That God continuously cares for creation was mentioned by two constituents of the National Council of Churches of Christ—the Disciples of Christ and the Presbyterian Church USA.[80] A fruitful approach to this principle is incorporating it into the call to stewardship so faith-filled people understand that they are cooperating with God by actions that avoid degrading the internal functioning of Earth. Distinguishing between God's role and humanity's is vital when addressing the notion of God's care. To suggest that God will intervene in creation as a cause among causes will make impossible a determination of how humans should act because of the uncertainty of how God is acting. Furthermore, positing God's intervention to correct human abuse might lead some believers to think that God will correct whatever they do or that they need not act because God will take care of whatever God desires.[81] By functioning cooperatively with ecological processes and the biosphere in ways that mitigate or avoid global warming, faith-filled people may consider themselves cooperators with God who sustains Earth and the entire universe in existence and calls it forth to its fullest possible expression.[82]

The National Council of Churches of Christ and the Evangelical Environmental Network underscored the principle that humans are called to participate in the redemption of the entirety of creation.[83] This principle can be developed within their memberships as a constructive embellishment to the role of humans as stewards who care for God's creation because they are motivated by the desire to participate in God's redemptive action. That God is working through Christ to redeem the entirety of creation is a divergent principle that these two partners along with the Conference of Catholic Bishops can embrace effectively.

God's presence in creation is mentioned by the American Baptist Church and the Catholic Bishops of the Columbia River watershed region,[84] but what this notion of the immanence of God in creation means must be made clear, since both also ascribe to the concept of the transcendence of God. The latter also emphasize the Catholic understanding of the sacramentality of creation—that the universe in its micro-to-macro dimensions manifests God's presence and activity. Both faith-based notions can be used to significant advantage when educating and motivating the membership of those partners.

Commitment to the covenant with God may provide considerable help in a campaign aimed at mitigating global warming. Though the Reformed Church of America and the Church of the Brethren articulated the belief that the covenant with God included all of creation,[85] the partners may wish to examine their traditions and consider endorsing this principle for use in the campaign.

Deepening the Public Theology

While the various partners have delved significantly into their traditions to identify meaningful theological foundations for reflecting and acting on global warming, more in-depth framing of reflection around the notions of environmental prudence, environmental temperance, and environmental justice may be helpful. Attention to environmental injustice and specifically environmental racism is especially crucial.[86]

Needing explicit definition and direction in a global warming campaign is the model of the human as the steward of God's creation who is responsible to God for caring for God's Earth. The virtue of prudence may help fill this need, and one of the sources the Partnership may consult is Thomas Aquinas. To his teachings we now turn.

According to Aquinas, prudence is the habit of being discreet,[87] a way of thinking that could be a mainstay of the Partnership when planning and guiding the national campaign. Being prudent requires choosing a means of action through a process of taking counsel, forming a good judgment, and commanding correctly. Taking counsel is an act of inquiry aimed at discovering the appropriate means toward achieving a goal.[88] Both the private good of the individual and the common good of groups to which the individual belongs are considered when seeking counsel. The good of the individual is impossible, Aquinas argued, unless the common good of others is assured.[89] Thus, the prudent individual considers what is good for one's self by being prudent about what is good for many.[90]

In the process of taking counsel from informed sources, a prudent individual discerns what is needed to sustain one's life, the life of one's neighbor, and the community to which the person belongs.[91] Judgment is made subsequently on the means most applicable for acting on other beings for the purpose of acquiring what is needed for human sustenance.[92] Command, the chief and final act in prudent decision-making, requires three considerations that have special significance for environmental ethics generally and global warming specifically: foresight, circumspection and caution.[93] Foresight assures that what is commanded in the present is fitting for the future.[94] Circumspection facilitates the choice of suitable means to an end in light of a combination of circumstances that may arise.[95] Caution is required to avoid evil through a firm understanding of good.[96] While this process does not assure a successful outcome, its uncertainty is lessened through the practice of prudent decision-making over time.[97]

This framework for the exercise of prudence suggests a systematic approach to addressing global warming that is motivated by the desire to care responsibly for God's creation. A link can be made from prudence to the partners' shared called to environmental justice to assure that humans and all living beings have access to a life-sustaining planet and to the particular goods they need absolutely to maintain themselves in their habitats. Linkage can also be made to environmental temperance by explicitly embracing the principle of avoiding waste and destruction of Earth that the Coalition on Environment and Jewish Life articulates. Key to this virtue is defining needs vs. wants, identifying ways of striving to exercise this virtue in all aspects of human life, and developing the humility that is needed to recognize and act on the dependence that humans have on other species, the air, the land, and bodies of water that are threatened by the effects of greenhouse gas emissions. A final link to developing the virtue of fortitude can provide the courage the partners and their constituents need to be steadfast in the months and years ahead as a national plan to mitigate global warming is developed, promoted, and implemented.

Conclusion

A life-sustaining climate is a common good that has been identified as a key moral concern by leaders of the world religions and organizations that profess to follow the faiths they represent. Bringing religious concerns into the public arena in the form of a well-developed public theology should raise awareness among believers and decision-makers to their responsibilities for taking action to mitigate the adverse effects that scientists have been predicting. A major effort by the constituents of the National Religious Partnership for the Environment to collaborate in addressing the phenomenon of global warming from foundational theological beliefs would contribute to the public discussion. As indicated in a review of seventy-four documents issued by the Partnership and its constituents individually and collaboratively, they share several religious principles that can serve as a basis for a public theology to undergird a national campaign on global warming aimed at encouraging dialogue and action at all levels of social, economic, and political life. Other religious principles that are unique to one or more partners can be used effectively by those constituents to particularize the national campaign for their followers so they are provided by the deepest possible meaning for thinking and acting in morally responsible ways. Some principles need more clarity and in-depth development in order to address the issue of global warming in meaningful and relevant ways. Essential to this task is calling upon the theological resources of each tradition to the fullest possible extent in order to provide the religious motivation for the planners, the implementers, and the faith-filled people on whom the partners will be calling for reflection and action.

Notes

1. David Hollenbach, *The Common Good and Christian Ethics* (New York: Cambridge University Press, 2002). Especially see chap 4 "Religion in Public" (pp. 87-112) and chap 8 "The Global Common Good" (pp. 212-44). Hollenbach weaves a theoretical framework for the common good based upon goods that should be held in common by all, the public role of religion, and the intellectual solidarity for rethinking urban poverty and globalization. Drawing on social analysis, moral philosophy, and theological ethics, Hollenbach charts new directions in both urban life and global society, argues that the division between the middle class and the poor in major cities and the challenges of globalization require a new commitment to the common good to which both religious believers and secular people must attend in solidarity, and proposes a positive vision of how a reconstructed understanding of the common good can lead to better lives for all people today.

2. Helpful essays addressing some of crucial theological questions pertaining to the common good are provided in *Religion, Ethics and the Common Good*, a collection of papers given at the 1996 meeting of the College Theology Society and edited by James Donahue and M. Theresa (Mystic, CT: Twenty-Third Publications, 1996). See also *Principles of Catholic Social Teaching*, ed. David A. Boileau (Milwaukee, WI: Marquette University Press, 1998); *In Search of the Common Good*, ed. Dennis P. McCann and Patrick D. Miller (New York: T & T Clark, 2005) which focuses on the meaning of the common good and identifies resources in Christian theology, biblical studies, and ethics that contribute to our understanding of the concept; *Common Good, Uncommon Questions: A Primer in Moral Theology*, ed. Timothy Backous and William C. Graham (Collegeville, MN: Liturgical Press, 1997), a collection of Scripture passages, current Church teaching, and contemporary reflections on several moral issues in search of the common good. An anthology of essays critically and constructively examining the promise and problems of the controversial movement aimed at pressuring the electronic and print media to promote and improve the quality of public life rather that merely reporting on it is *The Idea of Public Journalism*, ed. Theodore L. Glasser (New York: Guilford Press, 1999); see also *Mixed News: The Public/Civic/Communitarian Journalism Debate*, ed. Jay Black (Mahwah, NJ: Lawrence Erlbaum Associates, 1997). Examining the common good from an economic perspective are essays in *The Common Good and U.S. Capitalism*, ed. Oliver F. Williams and John W. Houck (Lanham, MD: University Press of America, 1987) which were co-published by arrangement with the Notre Dame Center for Ethics and Religious Values in Business.

3. Many monographs have been published on specific issues in relation to the common good. Among those addressing genetic manipulation is Karen Peterson-Iyer's *Designer Children: Reconciling Genetic Technology, Feminism, and Christian Faith* (Cleveland, OH: Pilgrim Press, 2004). Health care issues are covered by Jose I. Lavastida, Jose I. in *Health Care and the Common Good: A Catholic Theory of Justice* (Lanham, MD: University Press of America, 2000), and Charles J. Dougherty, *Back to Reform: Values, Markets, and the Health Care System* (New York: Oxford University Press, 1996). Political and economic approaches are addressed in Brian Stiltner's *Catholic Perspective in Religion and the Common Good: Catholic Contributions to Building Community in a Liberal Society* (Lanham, MD: Rowman & Littlefield, 1999), Raymond W. Y. Kao and Rowland R. Kao's *Entrepreneurism: A Philosophy and a Sensible Alternative for the Market Economy* (London: Imperial College Press, 2002); and, Albino Barrera's *Modern Catholic Social Documents and Political Economy* (Washington, DC: Georgetown University Press, 2001). Francis N. Lovett deals with the concept from an environmental perspective in *National Parks: Rights and the Common Good* (Lanham, MD: Rowman & Littlefield, 1998). A feminist perspective is advocated in *Aquinas, Feminism, and the Common Good* (Washington, DC: Georgetown University Press, 2004) by Susanne M. DeCrane who retrieves and reconstructs Thomas Aquinas' thinking for application today). Edward P. DeBerri and James E. Hug (with Peter J. Henriot and Michael J. Schultheis) remind Catholics about common good discourse in their tradition in *Catholic Social Teaching: Our Best Kept Secret*, 4th ed. rev. and expanded, (New York: Orbis Books, 2003). Official Church statements on the common good include *The Common Good and the Catholic Church's Social Teaching*, a statement by the Catholic Bishops' Conference of England & Wales (London: The Conference, 1996).
4. An excellent summation of Catholic teaching by several popes on the notion of the common good of humans appears in Pope John XXIII's encyclical letter *Mater et Magistra*, Vatican City, 15 May 1961. At #65, he calls for public authority to have "a sane view of the common good" by taking into account "all those social conditions which favor the full development of human personality." He also considers it "altogether vital that the numerous intermediary bodies and corporate enterprises... loyally collaborate in pursuit of their own specific interests and those of the common good." At #80, he addresses the demands of the common good on the international level—the "universal common good"—and calls for "the avoidance of all forms of unfair competition between the economies of different countries; the fostering of mutual collaboration and good will; and effective co-operation in the development of economically less advanced communities." The Pope's teachings are geared toward the common good of the human community. Lucia A. Silecchia provides an impressive overview of the Catholic hierarchy's understanding of the environment as a common good through the mid-1990s at pp. 690-712 in "Environmental Ethics from the Perspective of NEPA and Catholic Social Teaching: Ecological Guidance for the 21st Century," *William & Mary Environmental Law and Policy Review* 28 (2004): 659-797.
5. William C. French, "Catholicism and the Common Good of the Biosphere" in *Ecology of the Spirit: Religious Reflection and Environmental Consciousness*, ed. Michael Barnes, 177-94 (Lanham, MD: University Press of America, 1994).
6. However promising Aquinas's thinking about the common good of the biosphere is, French contends, the medieval theologian's teachings about the universal common good is often "overwhelmed" by another organizing principle that he describes as "the absolute superiority of rational human life over all lesser creatures," a principle for which he sees little room in theological ethics today. Indeed, Aquinas's understanding of the human suffered from the absence of knowledge during his time of the cosmological-biological evolutionary process out of which humans emerged, an understanding that tempers our current thinking about humans in relation to other species and abiota. However, French does not factor into his evaluation of Aquinas's thinking the severe restrictions he placed on how humans are intended to function in relation to other creatures because of their mutual relationship to God and humans' intended goal of eternal happiness with God, as demonstrated in Jame Schaefer, "The Virtuous Cooperator: Modeling the Human in an Age of Ecological Degradation," *Worldviews: Environment, Culture, Religion* 7.1-2 (March 2003): 171-195.
7. Thomas Aquinas, *Summa theologiae* 1|2.19.10; he used the phrase *bonum commune*. See also *Summa theologiae* 1.61.3 and *Summa contra Gentiles* 1.70.4 and 3.69.17. For Aquinas, the common good of the universe is its integrity that results from the order and composition of all its parts as discernable from *Summa contra Gentiles* 3.94.11, *De potentia Dei* 1.6.1, and *Summa theologiae* 1.115.3.
8. See, for example, Aquinas, *Summa contra Gentiles* 1.85.4, *De potentia Dei* 1.6.1,and *Summa theologiae* 1.103.7). All constituents benefit from being ordered to the whole, he taught in *Summa*

theologiae 1|2.19.10, because the entirety of parts ordered hierarchically to one another to constitute a whole is the common good of all parts. In the disputed question on truth, *De veritate* 5.3, Aquinas paralleled his treatment of the common good of the universe with the common good of citizens of a particular society. He explained that a common element to be found in the way God governs things in the universe and a king rules a kingdom is the primacy of the common good over the good of the individual.

9. For example, see Aquinas, *Summa theologiae* 1|2.109.3 and 2|2.26.3.
10. Aquinas, *Summa theologiae* 2|2.26.3. For Aquinas, even stones and other things without knowledge are inclined toward the common good in at least a natural way (*Summa theologiae* 2|2.26.3), and each is more strongly inclined to the common good of the whole than to itself (*Summa theologiae* 1.60.5 and 2|2.26.3 ad 2). At the root of this natural appetite for the common good is the natural inclination that each creature has for God who is the absolute common good of all creatures (*Summa theologiae* 1.60.5 ads 3-5 and 2|2.26.3).
11. Aquinas, *Summa contra Gentiles* 3.24.8 and *Summa theologiae* 1.57.2.
12. Aquinas, *Summa contra Gentiles* 3.24.8.
13. Aquinas, *Summa theologiae* 1|2.9.1.
14. Aquinas, *De potentia Dei* 4.2 ad 29.
15. Aquinas, *De veritate* 5.2.
16. Aquinas, *Summa theologiae* 1.11.3.
17. Joseph Legrand, *L'univers et l'homme dans la philosophie de Saint Thomas*, 2 vols. (Brussels: L'Édition Universelle, 1946), 1:40.
18. Aquinas, *Summa contra Gentiles* 2.68.6.
19. God's ordering of things to one another to achieve the good of the whole universe is described by Aquinas as the good and the best in the universe (*Summa contra Gentiles* 2.39.7; cf. 2.45.9, 3.69.17, and 3.144.10; and *Summa theologiae* 1.22.1-2), the greatest good in created things (*Summa contra Gentiles* 2.44.2), and the highest good in the universe (*Summa theologiae* 1.15.2). The integrity of all created beings is also described as the ultimate and noblest perfection in things (*Summa contra Gentiles* 2.45.100). All parts of the universe are ordered to the perfection of the whole (*Summa contra Gentiles* 3.112.8). When all parts function in innately appropriate and relational ways as a totality of interconnected parts, the universe is most perfect, it reflects the goodness of God, and it manifests God's glory (*Summa theologiae* 1.65.2). The interactive order of all things to constitute the universe is, according to Aquinas, the greatest perfection and the most beautiful attribute of creation because it reflects the goodness and wisdom of God (*Compendium theologiae* 102). All mutually distinct and ordered forms of things that constitute the universe exist in the mind of God, and it is by their functioning in ways intended by God that they constitute the greatest beauty and perfection that is possible for a created entity (e.g., *Summa contra Gentiles* 2.42.6; *Summa theologiae* 1.2.3, 1.4.2, 1.13.2).
20. John Wright, *The Order of the Universe in the Theology of St. Thomas Aquinas* (Rome: Gregorian University Press, 1957), 87.
21. The Assisi Declarations are accessible from the United Nations Environmental Program web site at http://www.nyo.unep.org/eaf/eafadec.pdf.
22. Access this statement from the National Religious Partnership for the Environment site at http://www.nrpe.org/openletter.html.
23. Pope John Paul II, *The Ecological Crisis: A Common Responsibility*, Message on the World Day of Peace, Vatican City, 1 January 1990. He wove into his earlier and later statements, messages, and encyclicals his concern for the environment from a theological perspective, often stressing the harm environmental abuse poses to the dignity of the human individual and family. A homily entitled "We Must Be the Custodians of Nature" which the Pope gave on 12 November 2000 during a mass he celebrated with thousands of farmers from around the world is accessible from http://www.catholicculture.org/docs/doc_view.cfm?recnum=3260. Other documents Pope John Paul II and other pontiffs have issued are accessible from http://www.inee.mu.edu/ under the title "Catholic Church on Ecological Degradation," an Honors Program Project by Heather R. Whittington, my student in Theology 170 Theology and the Natural Sciences in Spring 2004.
24. John Chryssavgis, "Bartholomew, Ecumenical Patriarch (b. 1940)," http://www.clas.ufl.edu/users/bron/PDF--Christianity/Chryssavgis--Orthodox percent20Patriarch percent20Bartholomew.pdf, accessed 15 June 2005. Among the Patriarch's initiatives was a proclamation in 2002 that refusal to treat the natural environment properly as "a gift of communion with God and one another as humanity's original sin," the formation of an international Religion, Science, and Environment

Committee to raise public awareness and promote interdisciplinary, inter-confessional, and inter-religious dialogue.
25. Pope John Paul II and Patriarch Bartholomew I of Constantinople, "Roman Catholic-Eastern Orthodox Joint Declaration on the Environment: We Are Still Betraying the Mandate God Has Given Us," Venice, Italy, 10 June 2002.
26. Drafted by representatives of the Presbyterian Church USA, the Greek Orthodox Archdiocese of America, the Christian Methodist Church in Louisiana and Mississippi, and the Evangelical Lutheran Church of America and scholars, "God's Earth is Sacred: An Open Letter to Church and Society in the United States" was signed and issued in February 2005 (accessible from http://www.ncccusa.org./news/14.02.05theologicalstatement.html). Also see "Statement by Religious Leaders at the Summit on Environment" signed in June 1991 by representatives of the World Council of America, the Rabbinical Council of America, the Bishop and Primate of the Episcopal Church, the National Council of Churches of Christ, the United States Conference of Catholic Bishops, the American Baptist Church, the Greek Orthodox Archdiocese of North and South America, the President of Hebrew Union College, the Reconstructionist Rabbinical College, the Turtle Clan of the Onondaga Nation, the Cathedral of St. John the Divine, the National Baptist Convention, Church Women United, Jewish Theological Seminary, the Crystal Cathedral, World Vision U.S.A., Council of Bishops of the United Methodist Church, and the Southern Baptist Convention.
27. The U.S. Catholic Bishops' November 1991 "Renewing the Earth: An Invitation to Reflection and Action on Environment in Light of Catholic Social Teaching" was among the first statements issued but is not included in this overview of the documents specifically on energy and global warming that were provided by the National Religious Partnership for the Environment and two of its constituents' Interfaith Energy and Climate Campaign. That statement and others issued by Catholic bishops are accessible from http://www.inee.mu.edu/ after clicking on the Catholic Church button.
28. COEJI published the manual entitled *To Till and to Tend: A Guide to Jewish Environmental Study and Action* that is used widely among congregations.
29. From tentative beginnings in the mid 1980s, IFEES has established itself as an internationally recognized body that articulates the Islamic position on environmental matters, engaging in research, teaching, and setting up an experimental center on land use, organic farming, and the development of alternative technology. From its web site (http://www.ifees.org/), IFEES indicates that it "networks world-wide with NGOs, international organisations, academic bodies and grass roots organisations and invites collaboration from organisations and individuals from all persuasions who are also dedicated to the maintenance of the Earth as a healthy habitat for future generations of humankind as well as other living beings." Accessed 15 June 2005.
30. See, for example, the document issued by the National American Coalition for Christianity and Ecology from http://www.nacce.org/index.html on which the establishment of a JPIC ministry within the National Episcopal Church was announced, and search the www to discover many similar initiatives.
31. Alaska Native Knowledge Network http://www.ankn.uaf.edu/iksgraph.html; Honor the Earth http://honorearth.com/; Indigenous Environmental Network http://www.ienearth.org/; National Environmental Coalition of Native Americans http://oraibi.alphacdc.com/necona/; Native American Fish and Wildlife Society http://www.nafws.org/; Native Americans and the Environment http://cnie.org/NAE/ ; Navajo Dinèè CARE http://dinecare.indigenousnative.org/; Akwesasne Task Force on the Environment (Mohawk) http://www.slic.com/atfe/atfe.htm; Columbia River Pastoral Letter Project http://www.columbiariver.org/; Earth Ministry http://www.earthministry.org/; Episcopal Diocese of Minnesota Environmental Stewardship Commission http://www.env-steward.com/; Lutheran Earthkeeping Network of the Synods (LENS) http://www.webofcreation.org/lens/index.html; National Conference of Catholic Bishops/US Catholic Conference: USCC Environmental Justice Program http://www.nccbuscc.org/sdwp/ejp/index.htm; National Council of Churches (NCC) Eco-Justice Working Group http://www.webofcreation.org/ncc/Workgrp.html; National Religious Partnership for the Environment (NRPE) http://www.nrpe.org/; Theological Education to Meet the Ecological Challenge (TEMEC) http://www.center1.com/crle/temec/temec.html; Theology Library: Environment http://www.mcgill.pvt.k12.al.us/jerryd/cm/environ.htm ; Unitarian Universalist Seventh Principle Project http://www.uuaspp.org/; Web of Creation http://www.webofcreation.org/home2.html; Coalition for Environment and Jewish Life (COEJL) http://www.coejl.org/; Northwest Jewish Environmental Project http://www.nwjep.org/.
32. See the National Religious Partnership for the Environment's web site (http://www.nrpe.org/) which describes the organization's activities as "integrating care for God's creation throughout religious

33. The Alliance has also prepared practical suggestions for believers to join in mitigating global warming. See http://www.arcworld.org/, accessed 17 June 2005.
34. The *Encyclopedia of Religion and Nature*, edited by Bron R. Taylor (New York: Continuum Press, 2005) highlights reflections from the world religions that relate positively toward the natural environment.
35. An overview of the ten volumes and the introductory essay by the Harvard conference organizers and Bucknell University Religious Studies professors Mary Evelyn Tucker and John Grim entitled "The Challenge of the Environmental Crisis" are accessible from http://environment.harvard.edu/religion/publications/books/book_series/cswr/index.html.
36. The Forum on Religion and Ecology, http://environment.harvard.edu/religion/main.html, accessed 15 June 2005.
37. That religions face a serious challenge when addressing the environmental crisis is acknowledged by the conference organizers and Forum leaders. According to Mary Evelyn Tucker and John Grim in "Religions of the World and Ecology: Discovering the Common Ground" accessible from http://environment.harvard.edu/religion/information/index.html, accessed 15 June 2005: "it is increasingly clear that the environmental crisis presents a serious challenge to the world's religions...since many of these religions have traditionally been concerned with the paths of personal salvation which frequently emphasize other worldly goals and reject this world as corrupting. How to adapt religious teachings to this task of revaluing nature so as to prevent its destruction marks a significant new phase in religious thought..... How to utilize the insights of the world's religions is a task of formidable urgency."
38. "Insights: Joint Science Academies' Global Response to Climate Change," *Environmental News Service*, 7 June 2005, http://www.ens-newswire.com/ens/jun2005/2005-06-07-insaca,asp, accessed 8 June 2005.
39. United Nations Intergovernmental Panel on Climate Change, "Safeguarding the Oxone Layer and the Global Climate System: Issues Related to Hydrofluorocarbons and Perfluorocarbons," IPCC Secretariat, April 2005, http://www.ipcc.ch, accessed 16 June 2005. Among the initiatives recommended are moving toward renewable energy sources to generate electricity, development of energy-efficient technologies and low- and zero-carbon energy supplies, reduction of large emissions of greenhouse gases, subsidies for biofuels, cap-and-trade systems for carbon emissions, and greater financial and technical assistance by developed countries to vulnerable countries.
40. See, for example, Michael Coren's examples in "The Science Debate Behind Climate Change: Forecasting the Future Remains a Contentious Exercise," CNN, 8 April 2005, http://www.cnn..com/2005/TECH/science/04/08/earth.science, accessed 16 June 2005.
41. The International Climate Change Taskforce, *Meeting the Climate Challenge*, January 2005, http://www.americanprogress.org/site/pp.asp?c=biJRJ80VF&b=306 (accessed 16 June 2005). cites economic threats caused by global warming but says "the social and human costs are likely to be even greater, encompassing mass loss of life, the spread or exacerbation of diseases, dislocation of populations, geo-political instability, and a pronounced decrease in the quality of life." The report states that if nothing is done, the Greenland and Antarctic ice sheets will eventually melt, causing island nations and highly populated coastal areas to be destroyed. Irreversible damage to the Amazon rainforests and coral reefs would occur. Also, the Gulf Stream would disappear. For these reasons, the report argues that climate protection must be seen in the context of national security and public health.
42. "Green Cities Declaration," The San Francisco Urban Environmental Accords, 5 June 2005, http://www.wed2005.org/3.1.php, accessed 16 June 2005. The Urban Accords are also accessible at http://www.urbanaccords.org.
43. "California Governor Orders Cuts in Global Warming Emissions," *Environmental News Service*, 2 June 2005, http://www.ens-newswire.com/ens/jun2005/2005-06-05.asp, accessed 6 June 2005.
44. Kyoto Protocol, http://unfccc.int/resource/docs/convkp/kpeng.html, accessed 6-5-05.
45. United Nations Intergovernmental Panel on Climate Change, "Climate Change 2001: The Scientific Basis," 2001, http://www.grida.no/climate/ipcc_tar/wg1/index.htm, accessed 16 June 2005.
46. "G8 Climate Plan of Action Delivers Little Change," *Environment News Service*, 8 July 2005, www.ens-newswire.com/ens/jul2005/2005-07-08-02.asp, accessed 9 July 2005.
47. Ibid.

48. I am grateful to Paul Gorman, Executive Director of the National Religious Partnership for the Environment, and Lindsay Moseley of the Interfaith Climate and Energy Campaign sponsored by two of the partners (the National Council of Churches of Christ and the Coalition on Environment and Jewish Life) for providing the seventy-four documents in various formats issued by the Partnership's constituents individually or collaboratively in which they express their respective beliefs for advocating changes in the public arena to mitigate and further prevent the effects of global warming, identifying their shared beliefs upon which to build a public theology, and suggesting where their theological rationale can be strengthened as they move into their collaborative effort. Paul Heidebrecht, a doctoral student in Religious Studies and my Teaching Assistant during the Fall 2004 semester facilitated the analysis of these documents.

49. Statements focusing on the need for a religious response to global warming have been issued separately by the four partners and by several constituents of the National Council of Churches of Christ: American Baptist Church, Church of the Brethren, Disciples of Christ, Episcopal Church, Evangelical Church of America, Religious Society of Friends, Presbyterian Church USA, Reformed Church of America, Reformed Church of America, and United Methodist Church. Collaborative efforts by partners from 2001 to 2004 include a number of documents and educational materials issued by the NRPE's Interfaith Climate and Energy Campaign pertaining to energy, climate change, power plants, and fuel economy. Another collaborative effort is a study guide on global warming entitled "The Cry of Creation: A Call for Climate Justice" by the National Council of Churches of Christ and the Coalition on the Environment and Jewish Life.

50. In *The Common Good and Christian Ethics*, Hollenbach counters astutely this thesis proffered by Samuel P. Huntington in "The Clash of Civilizations" *Foreign Affairs* 72 (Summer 1993): 22-48. At pp. 96-98, Hollenbach points to efforts by Baptist Reverend Martin Luther King, Jr., Hindu leader Mahatma Gandhi, Catholic bishop Oscar Romero of San Salvador, Archbishop Desmond Tutu of South Africa, Rigoberta Menchú of Guatemala, Buddhist religious leaders Samdech Preah Maha Ghosananda of Cambodia, Sulak Sivaraksa of Thailand and Thich Nhat Hanh of Vietnam, and others highlighted by R. Scott Appleby in *The Ambivalence of the Sacred: Religion, Violence and Reconciliation* (Lanham, MD: Rowman and Littlefield, 1999), chaps 4 and 7.

51. Hollenbach, *The Common Good and Christian Ethics*, 98-99.

52. Ibid., 108.

53. Ibid., 104. Hollenbach provides a traditional view of religious communities as offering answers to deep questions humans ask about the meaning of life, love, work and death and nurturing moral values and virtues that enable people to live according to that meaning.

54. Michael J. And Kenneth R. Himes, *Fullness of Faith: The Public Significance of Theology* (New York: Paulist, 1993), 1. The authors draw upon Martin Marty's thinking in *The Public Church* (New York: Crossroad, 1981). All three theologians were thinking about shared concerns and beliefs among Christians of different denominations, while I am expanding upon their definition to include Jewish congregations.

55. Hollenbach, "Public Theology in America: Some Questions for Catholicism after John Courtney Murray," *Theological Studies* 37 (1976): 290-303, 299. At p. 23 of *Fullness of Faith*, the Himeses point to the benefit of contributing to "the vitality of a democratic society" when organized religions enter the public debate. In *The Catholic Ethic and the Spirit of Capitalism* (New York: Free Press, 1993), 187, Michael Novak recognizes "the capacity to cooperate with others...in achieving ends that benefit society" as a significant attribute in the quest for social justice as locating the difference in social justice.

56. Himes, *Fullness of Faith*, 23. Ignoring the theological underpinnings for moral choices is problematic for these scholars. "One of the benefits of public theology is that it makes explicit the theological component of social ethics so believers can understand and test the coherence of their religious beliefs with their public policy decisions." At 25, they urge the expression of theological foundations for social action "in ways that reveal the deep biblical and theological roots of the concern.... A public theology helps to avoid the neglect of our biblical and theological tradition when we move to matters of social life. It provides the rich foundation available to the church for taking on the task of building a just and peaceful world."

57. Ibid., 26.

58. In "Public Catholicism: An American Prospect," *Theological Studies* 62 (2001): 701-29, theologian Thomas Hughson, S.J. appeals for a Catholic public theology that explicitly stresses the singularity of racial-social-environmental justice. The justice dimension of addressing environmental concerns has been strong in efforts initiated by the National Religious Partnership for the Environment.

59. Ibid, 703.

60. "Renewing the Face of the Earth: Global Climate Change and Energy Conservation Activities in the American Religious Community, 2004-2005," Interfaith Climate and Energy Campaign, not dated; "The Cry of Creation: Global Warming and Global Justice," not dated; "The Cry of Creation: A Call for Climate Justice,: Interfaith Climate and Energy Campaign, not dated; "Let There Be Light: Energy Conservation and God's Creation: An Open Letter to the President, the Congress, and the American People," Interfaith Climate and Energy Campaign, 18 May 2001; "Earth's Climate Embraces Us All: A Plea from Religion and Science for Action on Global Warming," Interfaith Climate and Energy Campaign, July 2004; "An Open Letter to President Bush Concerning America's Clean Air from 95 Christian Leaders," Interfaith Climate and Energy Campaign, 28 April 2004; "Sermon Ideas about Fuel Economy," Interfaith Climate and Energy Campaign, not dated; "Testimony of Paul Gorman at the U.S. Senate Committee on Commerce, Science, and Transportation Hearing on the Case for Climate Change Action," Interfaith Climate and Energy Campaign, 1 October 2003; "A Call for Power Plant Clean-up," Interfaith Climate and Energy Campaign, not dated; "Religious Leaders; Letter to Governor Granholm on the Fuel Economy of State Fleet Vehicles," Interfaith Climate and Energy Campaign, 15 September 2003; "What Should the Governor Drive?", Interfaith Climate and Energy Campaign, 15 September 2003; "Environmental Policy Platform," Coalition on the Environment and Jewish Life," 2004; "Jews, Jewish Texts, and Nature: A Brief History," Coalition on the Environment and Jewish Life, not dated; "The Columbia River Watershed: Caring for Creation and the Common Good," Catholic Bishops of the Columbia River Watershed Region, 2001; "Global Climate Change: A Plea for Dialogue, Prudence and the Common Good," U.S. Conference of Catholic Bishops, 2001; "Letter to U.S. Senators Concerning the Climate Stewardship Act," U.S. Conference of Catholic Bishops, 2004; "Heat Stroke: The Climate for Addressing Global Warming is Improving," Evangelical Environmental Network, 2004; "Resolution on President Carter's Proposed Energy Program," National Council of Churches, 1977; "Resolution in Support of Interreligious Program on Religion and Energy in the '80s," National Council of Churches, 1980; "The Oil Spill in Prince William Sound, Alaska, National Council of Churches, 1989; "God's Creation and Global Warming,:" National Council of Churches, 2000; "It's God's World: Christians, Care for Creation and Global Warming," National Council of Churches, 2002; "American Baptist Policy Statement on Energy," American Baptist Church, 1998; "American Baptist Resolution on Global Warming," American Baptist Church, 1991; "Resolution Concerning Energy," Disciples of Christ, 1977; "Executive Council Statement on Conservation-Based Energy Legislation," Episcopal Church, 2002; "Philadelphia Yearly Meeting Minute on Global Climate Change," Religious Society of Friends, 2000; "Philadelphia Yearly Meeting Minute on Concern for Energy Stewardship in Meeting Facilities and Households," Religious Society of Friends, 2003; "Policy Statement: Restoring Creation for Ecology and Justice," 1990; "General Synod Statement on Caring for Creation (Climate Change)," Reformed Church of America, 1998; "Energy Policy Statement," United Methodist Church, 2000.

61. The nine documents within those mentioned in the prior endnote that include this belief are "An Open Letter to President Bush Concerning America's Clean Air from 95 Christian Leaders," Interfaith Climate and Energy Campaign, 28 April 2004; "Local Events Talking Points, Sermon, Test Drives,: Interfaith Climate and Energy Campaign, 2002; "Jews, Jewish Texts, and Nature: A Brief History," Coalition on the Environment and Jewish Life, not dated; "Heat Stroke: The Climate for Addressing Global Warming is Improving," Evangelical Environmental Network, 2004; "American Baptist Policy Statement on Energy," American Baptist Church, 1998; "Resolution Concerning Energy," Disciples of Christ, 1977; "Executive Council Statement on Conservation-Based Energy Legislation," Episcopal Church, 2002; "Philadelphia Yearly Meeting Minute on Global Climate Change," Religious Society of Friends, 2000; "Philadelphia Yearly Meeting Minute on Concern for Energy Stewardship in Meeting Facilities and Households," Religious Society of Friends, 2003; "Policy Statement Restoring Creation for Ecology and Justice," Presbyterian Church USA, 1990; "Energy Policy Statement," United Methodist Church, 2000." The additional document stating this belief is "Global Warming Statement," Reformed Church of America, 1993.

62. In the undated "Jewish Environmental Values: The Dynamic Tension Between Nature and Human Needs," the Coalition on the Environment and Jewish Life cautioned about the unavoidable dynamic tension between the capacity to exercise control over nature and the duty to act toward the environment with a sense of fiduciary responsibility.

63. "*Bal Tashchit*: The Development of a Jewish Environmental Principle," Coalition on the Environment and Jewish Life, not dated.

64. Avoiding waste was stressed by the Interfaith Climate and Energy Campaign which issued "Religious Leaders' Letter to Governor Granholm on the Fuel Economy of State Fleet Vehicles" on

15 September 2003 and "What Should the Governor Drive?" 2003-2004. Attitudes and actions pertaining that are destructive of the planet were proscribed explicitly by "The Cry of Creation: A Call for Climate Justice," not dated; "On the Care of Creation: An Evangelical Declaration on the Care of Creation," Evangelical Environmental Network, not dated; "Life-Giving Breath of God: Protecting the Sacred Gift of Air," National Council of Churches, 2004.

65. "Renewing the Face of the Earth," Interfaith Climate and Energy Campaign, not dated; "The Cry of Creation: Global Warming and Global Justice," Interfaith Climate and Energy Campaign, not dated; "The Cry of Creation: A Call for Climate Justice," Interfaith Climate and Energy Campaign, not dated; "Earth's Climate Embraces Us All: A Plea from Religion and Science for Action on Global Warming," Interfaith Climate and Energy Campaign, July 2004; "An Interfaith Call for Global Climate Justice," Interfaith Climate and Energy Campaign, 8 July 2004; "Testimony of Paul Gorman at the U.S. Senate Committee on Commerce, Science, and Transportation Hearing on the Case for Climate Change Action," Interfaith Climate and Energy Campaign, 1 October 2003; "Toll-free Call-in Day to Promote Climate Stewardship," Interfaith Climate and Energy Campaign, 7 July 2004; "A Call for Power Plant Clean-up," Interfaith Climate and Energy Campaign, not dated; "An Open Letter to President Bush Concerning America's Clean Air from 95 Christian Leaders," Interfaith Climate and Energy Campaign, 28 April 2004; "Sermon Ideas about Fuel Economy," Interfaith Climate and Energy Campaign, not dated; "Religious Leaders' Letter to Governor Granholm on the Fuel Economy of State Fleet Vehicles," Interfaith Climate and Energy Campaign, 15 September 2003; "What Should the Governor Drive?" Interfaith Climate and Energy Campaign, 15 September 2003; "Environmental Policy Platform," Coalition on the Environment and Jewish Life, 2004; "Letter to U.S. Senators Concerning the Climate Stewardship Act," U.S. Conference of Catholic Bishops, 2004; "About the Environmental Justice Program," U.S. Conference of Catholic Bishops, not dated; "The 'What Would Jesus Drive' Leaders Statement on S. 139 and the Need for Action on Climate Change," Evangelical Environmental Network, not dated; "Resolution on President Carter's Proposed Energy Program," National Council of Churches, 1977; "Resolution in Support of Interreligious Program on Religion and Energy in the '80s," National Council of Churches, 1980; "God's Creation and Global Warming," National Council of Churches, 2000; "American Baptist Policy Statement on Energy," American Baptist Church, 1998; "Denominational Statement: Energy," Presbyterian Church USA, 1979; "Denominational Statement: Speaking Truth to Power (Energy)," Presbyterian Church USA, 1981; "General Synod Statement on Caring for Creation (Climate Change)," Reformed Church of America, 1998.

66. In "Public Catholicism," Hughson argues convincingly about the indispensable interconnection of racial, social and environmental justice. On the issue of treating racial justice explicitly and not within the category of social justice, he explains "while racial justice logically belongs within social justice as one of its subsets, explicit attention to racial injustice is essential to deal with the bias of White supremacy in American Catholic theology, pastoral teaching, and ecclesial practice." For further scholarly efforts on the need to address racial injustice in relation to environmental degradation, also see Bryan N. Massingale, "James Cone and Recent Catholic Episcopal Teaching on Racism," *Theological Studies* 61 (2001) 700-30 and "An Ethical Reflection Upon 'Environmental Racism': In the Light of Catholic Social Teaching" in *Challenge of Global Stewardship*, ed. Maura A. Ryan and Todd David Whitmore, 234-50 (Notre Dame IN: University of Notre Dame Press, 1997). Joan Nordquist provides a list of monographs, anthologies, and articles in *Environmental Racism and the Environmental Justice Movement: A Bibliography* (Santa Cruz, CA: Reference and Research Services, 1995).

67. "Renewing the Face of the Earth," Interfaith Climate and Energy Campaign, not dated; "The Cry of Creation: Global Warming and Global Justice," Interfaith Climate and Energy Campaign, not dated; "The Cry of Creation: A Call for Climate Justice," Interfaith Climate and Energy Campaign, not dated; "Earth's Climate Embraces Us All," Interfaith Climate and Energy Campaign, July 2004; "Testimony of Paul Gorman at the U.S. Senate Committee on Commerce, Science, and Transportation," 1 October 2003; "A Call for Power Plant Clean-Up," Interfaith Climate and Energy Campaign, not dated; "Jewish Environmental Values: The Dynamic Tension between Nature and Human Needs," Coalition on Environment and Jewish Life, not dated; "Jews, Jewish Texts, and Nature: A Brief History," Coalition on Environment and Jewish Life, not dated; "The Columbia River Watershed," Catholic Bishops of the Region, 2001; "The Moral Demands of the Energy Crisis," National Council of Churches, 1973; "Resolution Concerning Energy," Disciples of Christ, 1977; "Policy Statement: Hope for a Global Future," Presbyterian Church USA, 1996; "It's God's World;," National Council of Churches, 2002; "General Synod Statement on Caring

68. for Creation (Climate Change)", Reformed Church of America, 1998; "Energy Policy Statement," United Methodist Church, 2000.
68. "Renewing the Face of the Earth," Interfaith Climate and Energy Campaign, not dated; "The Cry of Creation: Global Warming and Global Justice," Interfaith Climate and Energy Campaign, not dated; "The Cry of Creation: A Call for Climate Justice," Interfaith Climate and Energy Campaign, not dated; "Let There be Light: Energy Conservation and God's Creation," 18 May 2001; "Earth's Climate Embraces Us All," Interfaith Climate and Energy Campaign, July 1004; "An Interfaith Call for Global Climate Justice, Interfaith Climate and Energy Campaign, 8 July 2004; "Testimony of Paul Gorman at the U.S. Senate Committee on Commerce, Science and Transportation,: Interfaith Climate and Energy Campaign, 1 October 2003; "A Call for Power Plant Clean-Up," Interfaith Climate and Energy Campaign, not dated; "An Open Letter to President Bush," Interfaith Climate and Energy Campaign, 28 April 2004; "Sermon Ideas about Fuel Economy," Interfaith Climate and Energy Campaign, not dated; "Environmental Policy Platform," Coalition on the Environment and Jewish Life, 2004; "The What Would Jesus Drive' Leaders' Statement," Evangelical Environmental Network, not dated.
69. Of the six documents imploring care for the environment out of love for fellow humans are the the Evangelical Environmental Network's "What Would Jesus Drive?" issued in 2002, "The 'What Would Jesus Drive' Leaders' Statement" on date unknown, "Jesus' Lordship and Our Transportation Choices: Resources for Preaching and Teaching" on date unknown, and ""Heat Stroke" issued in 2004. Also calling for love of neighbor are two constituents of the National Churches of Christ—the American Baptist Church's "American Baptist Resolution on Global Warming" in 1991 and the Presbyterian Church USA's "Policy Statement: Restoring Creation for Ecology and Justice" in 1990.
70. "Earth's Climate Embraces Us All: A Plea From Religion and Science for Action on Global Warming," Interfaith Climate and Energy Campaign, July 2004; "An Open Letter to President Bush Concerning America's Clean Air from 95 Christian Leaders," Interfaith Climate and Energy Campaign, 28 April 2004; "Sermon Ideas about Fuel Economy," Interfaith Climate and Energy Campaign, not dated; "Global Climate Change: A Plea for Dialogue, Prudence and the Common Good," 2001; "On the Care of Creation: An Evangelical Declaration on the Care of Creation," Evangelical Environmental Network, not dated; "God's Creation and Global Warming," National Council of Churches, 2000; "It's God's World: Christians, Care for Creation and Global Warming," National Council of Churches, 2004; "Policy Statement: Restoring Creation for Ecology and Justice," Presbyterian Church USA, 1990.
71. For example, see "An Open Letter to President Bush Concerning America's Clean Air from 95 Christian Leaders," Interfaith Climate and Energy Campaign, 18 April 2004; and, "Sermon Ideas about Fuel Economy," Interfaith Climate and Energy Campaign, not dated.
72. "On the Care of Creation: An Evangelical Declaration on the Care of Creation," Evangelical Environmental Network, not dated; "Scripture Resources," Evangelical Environmental Network, not dated; "It's God's World: Christians, Care for Creation and Global Warming," National Council of Churches of Christ, 2002; "Life-Giving Breath of God: Protecting the Sacred Gift of Air," National Council of Churches of Christ, 2004; and, "Global Warming Statement" and "Climate Change Update by the Commission on Christian Action," Reformed Church of America, 1993 and 1998 respectively.
73. In the undated "Jews, Jewish Texts, and Nature: A Brief History," the Coalition on Environment and Jewish Life stipulated the belief that individual rights should be subordinated to communal responsibilities. The Conference of Catholic Bishops underscored the need to attend to the common good and especially the good of the poor in "About the Environmental Justice Program," not dated. Attending prudently to the universal common good that included other-than-humans was underscored by the Conference of Catholic Bishops in "Global Climate Change: A Plea for Dialogue, Prudence and the Common Good," 2001, and in "Letter to U.S. Senators Concerning the Climate Stewardship Act," 2004. The bishops of the Columbia River watershed also expressed concern for the universal common good in "The Columbia River Watershed," 2001.
74. "Global Climate Change: A Plea for Dialogue, Prudence, and the Common Good," A Statement of the United States Conference of Catholic Bishops, Washington, D.C. 15 June 2001. See especially pp. 11, 13, and 14 where the bishops call for "a civil dialogue and prudent and constructive action to protect God's precious gift of the earth's atmosphere with a sense of genuine solidarity and justice for all God's children." See also "Renewing the Earth," 5, under "Catholic Social Teaching and Environmental Ethics" where the bishops promote "an ethics of solidarity promoting cooperation and a just structure of sharing in the world community."

75. The Coalition on Environment and Jewish Life articulated this principle explicitly as *Bal Tashchit* in the undated "*Bal Tashchit:* The Development of a Jewish Environmental Principle," while the Presbyterian Church USA expressed the need to examine patterns of consumption in "Denominational Statement: Energy," in 1979.
76. Humility was mentioned by the Interfaith Climate and Energy Campaign on behalf of the National Council of Churches of Christ and the Coalition on Environment and Jewish Life in "The Cry of Creation: A Call for Climate Justice," whereas an appeal for prudence appeared in the Campaign's "Earth's Climate Embraces Us All," July 2004. An in-depth exploration of these concepts by the Partnership has yet to be accomplished.
77. For example, see Aquinas, *Summa theologiae* 2|2.161.1, 6.
78. Aquinas, *Summa theologiae* 1|2.57.4-6, 58.4 and 2|2.47.7.
79. "Policy Statement: Restoring Creation for Ecology and Justice," Presbyterian Church USA, 1990.
80. "Resolution Concerning Energy," Disciples of Christ, 1977; "Policy Statement: Restoring Creation for Ecology and Justice," 1990 and "Policy Statement: Hope for a Global Future," 1996, both issued by the Presbyterian Church USA.
81. To posit God as intervening in the natural functioning of the universe also poses other problems, including filling God into gaps of scientific knowledge and reducing divine activity to a material level.
82. Systematic theologian John F. Haught expresses well the joyful anticipation of the future unfolding of the universe in light of the past. See especially *The Promise of Nature: Ecology and Cosmic Purpose* (New York: Paulist Press, 1993).
83. "It's God's World," National Council of Churches of Christ, 2002; and, "What Would Jesus Drive?" Evangelical Environmental Network, 2002.
84. "The Columbia River Watershed," Catholic Bishops of the Region, 2001; and, "American Baptist Policy Statement on Energy," American Baptist Church, 1998.
85. "Climate Change Update by the Commission on Christian Action," Reformed Church of America, 1998; and, "General Board Resolution on Global Warming and Atmospheric Degradation, Church of the Brethren, 1991.
86. See, for example, the Bryan Massingale's alerts in "James Cone and Recent Catholic Episcopal Teaching on Racism," and "An Ethical Reflection Upon 'Environmental Racism."
87. Aquinas, *Summa theologiae* 1|2.61.2.
88. Aquinas, *Summa theologiae* 1|2.14.1, 57.6; also *Summa theologiae* 2|2.47.1-2 and 8.
89. Aquinas, *Summa theologiae* 2|2.47.10.
90. Ibid. Also see *Summa theologiae* 1.22.1 where Aquinas discussed God's providence as prudence by ordering all things in the universe to their ends. This connection serves to underscore the need for humans to reason correctly by ordering all their actions toward their ultimate end in God, a principle to which the four partners seem to ascribe.
91. Aquinas, *Summa theologiae* 1|2.65.1; also see *Summa theologiae* 1|2.57.4-6, 2|2.47.2 and 8.
92. Aquinas, *Summa theologiae* 2|2.47.8 and 1|2.57.6.
93. Aquinas, *Summa theologiae* 2|2.47.8; also see *Summa theologiae* 2|2.47.9 and 1|2.57.6.
94. Aquinas, *Summa theologiae* 2|2.49.6, 55.7.
95. Aquinas, *Summa theologiae* 2|2.49.7.
96. Aquinas, *Summa theologiae* 2|2.49.8.
97. Aquinas, *Summa theologiae* 2|2.49.5. In *Summa contra Gentiles* 3.122, Aquinas cautioned that developing the habit of being prudent requires considerable education and practice over a long period of time. Any person who has the ability to reason is competent to have prudence in proportion to the person's rationality, he explained in *Summa theologiae* 2|2.47.12.

Three Gorges be Dammed: The Philosophical Roots of Environmentalism in China

David L. Kenley

Anyone who has visited a Chinese-style garden is well aware of the beauty and naturalness exemplified in this traditional art form. These gardens are, many believe, sacred spaces that represent harmony between man and nature. A quick search through any bookstore will turn up titles such as *Zen in Your Garden*, *The Tao of Gardening*, and *Feng Shui Garden*.[1] Apparently, many customers believe that Chinese and other Asians have a spiritual connection with their gardens and with nature in general.

Despite these stereotypes, the past century has witnessed rampant environmental degradation throughout East Asia. As a latecomer to industrialization, China is currently feeling the effects of resource depletion. Statistics show that China is now the world's largest consumer of grain, meat, coal, and steel.[2] Not surprisingly, China is also experiencing the pollution that accompanies industrialization and consumerism. According to the World Health Organization, of the ten most polluted cities in the world, seven of them are in China.[3] Deforestation, dust storms, and smog affect millions of Chinese citizens.

Nevertheless, China's environmental problems are not simply the product of recent industrialization. Mao Zedong's revolution also had terrible consequences for China's environment.[4] Mao believed that man must conquer nature, and under his leadership, China's rivers, farms, and frontier regions suffered terribly. Mao and his associates advocated nonsensical farming techniques and forced large-scale human migration. By the time of his death in 1976, his "war against nature" had left much of China's ecology in ruins.

Ironically, Mao failed to accomplish one of his most lofty goals: damming the Yangzi River in Central China's scenic Three Gorges region. In a possible attempt to surpass Mao, subsequent political leaders have determined to build the Three Gorges Dam, despite the vociferous cries of environmental activists from around the world. Once completed, the resulting reservoir will cover nearly 450 square miles and may lead to the extinction of 75 percent of the local vertebrate species.[5]

In the past decade, however, China has seen more than simply a growth in consumerism and industrialism.[6] One other ism—environmentalism—is also spreading across the Chinese empire. Opponents of the Three Gorges Dam, including Non-Governmental

Organizations (NGOs) both within and outside China, are becoming more vocal and influential.[7]

How do China-watchers account for this apparent growth in environmentalism? Is this simply a fad that is sweeping through China? Are Chinese celebrities and intellectuals merely aping their Western counterparts? To make such suggestions not only demeans the efforts of Chinese activists, it also belittles the seriousness of China's environmental woes. China's ecological problems are severe and Chinese citizens from all social groups are reacting to these problems with genuine concern and fear.[8] Furthermore, the values of modern environmentalists are deeply rooted in traditional Chinese philosophy and religion. The purpose of this essay is to investigate these roots.

Several individuals have attempted to integrate Chinese religion into the modern environmental movement. For example, the Center for the Study of World Religions at Harvard recently sponsored a series of conferences to bring together over 700 scholars, religious leaders, and environmental activists.[9] Several of those that participated were experts in Chinese philosophy, religion, and intellectual history. One result of these conferences was the publication of three separate edited volumes containing essays analyzing the relationship between Chinese environmentalism and religion.[10] The essays are rich, varied, and stimulating, but for the non-China specialist, they can also be rather complex and unfocused. Furthermore, the essays are divided into three categories: Confucianism, Buddhism, and Daoism. This approach makes it difficult for the reader to appreciate the interconnectedness of these philosophies as they relate to the environment. As intellectual historians have long argued, the three schools of thought form a syncretic whole for most Chinese individuals, and therefore the three-volume division is somewhat artificial.

While Buddhism, Islam, and Christianity have all had a tremendous impact on Chinese history, each of these belief systems originated in South and Southwest Asia and was imported into China. Confucianism and Daoism (Taoism), on the other hand, are indigenous to China. Both Confucianism and Daoism have influenced social structures, political structures, and intellectual traditions throughout China's long history and will no doubt continue to have an influence on China's future. By looking specifically at what these traditions teach about self discipline, harmony, and activism, this essay will evaluate the usefulness of Confucianism and Daoism for China's environment.[11] Within these three areas, Confucianism and Daoism contain teachings that can have both a positive and a negative impact on China's environmental movement.

Relevant Teachings of Confucianism

In order to understand the environmental implications of Confucianism, it is necessary first to have a basic understanding of the philosophy. Kung Fuzi, or "Confucius," was born in 551 BCE. China at the time was wracked by civil war as various feudal states fought with one another. Confucius, frustrated with the chaos, sought to develop an intellectual framework for peace. By emphasizing *ren* (translated as humanity or benevolence), Confucius believed society could overcome the greed and cruelty that seemed ubiquitous.

Though *ren* formed the basis of his philosophy, Confucius' teachings are far more complex than this one word might suggest. For example, Confucius believed in a hierarchical, structured society in which each individual played an important role. Rulers, fathers, husbands, and older brothers each had a set of obligations and responsibilities to follow. Subjects, sons, wives, and younger brothers also had obligations and responsibilities. The key, Confucius taught, was for each of these individuals to understand his or her position and act accordingly. When each person played his or her (but usually his) appropriate role, acting with *ren*, society would function smoothly and harmoniously. Those individuals who most completely developed *ren*-based relationships were called "gentlemen" (*junzi*). Without enough such gentlemen, chaos was inevitable.

Despite his emphasis on hierarchy, Confucius' teachings also have an element of egalitarianism. While gentlemen sit atop Confucius' ideal government structure, the true gentleman is made, not born. Becoming a gentleman requires discipline, education, and self-control. In other words, it requires hard work. All individuals, Confucius taught, should strive to become gentlemen.

Confucius, perhaps more than any other single individual, has influenced Chinese history. Following his death, many of Confucius' disciples recorded his teachings in the *Analects*. These teachings, together with subsequent commentaries, formed the basis of China's intellectual cannon for over two millennia. Social advancement, including the opportunity to become a government official, depended on an individual's ability to learn and master these Confucian classics.

The influence of Confucianism has waxed and waned over the past two thousand years. For instance, during the Song Dynasty (960-1279) intellectuals reinvigorated the study of Confucianism, creating what historians have called Neo-Confucianism. Like their predecessor, Neo-Confucians emphasized *ren*, but they were more concerned with finding meaning in life and human existence. Intellectuals from this period sought to answer metaphysical questions regarding man and his relation to the cosmos. Life, they decided, was not illusory and ephemeral, as some religions teach, but was real and significant. Furthermore, the true Confucian should seek to solve the problems of this world. As Fan Zhongyan, a Neo-Confucian, explained, "the true scholar should be the first to become anxious about the world's troubles and the last to enjoy its happiness."[12] In short, like the original Confucians, the Neo-Confucian scholars emphasized cultivation, discipline, and self-control.

During the twentieth century, Confucianism and Neo-Confucianism came under sustained attack by intellectuals of all political stripes. Instead of turning to Confucianism for answers to China's social and political woes, intellectuals derided Confucianism for being backward and un-modern. With the eventual Communist victory in China, it appeared as if Confucianism was truly dead. However, Confucianism has proven to be more long lasting than many predicted. Though no longer part of the official curricula, Confucianism still has a tremendous influence on Chinese society. For example, the emphasis on academic success and self-improvement remains a hallmark of Chinese culture. Some have even credited the phenomenal economic growth in East Asia to "Confucian Capitalism." If the essence of Confucianism is self-discipline, harmony, and activism, then it appears the philosophy is alive and well in China today.

Confucianism and Self-Discipline

As is evidenced in his emphasis on the gentleman, Confucius believed in the necessity of self-discipline. The difference between the gentleman and the average man,

Confucius claimed, was education and hard work. "By nature men are pretty much alike," he wrote, "it is learning and practice that set them apart."[13] The challenge, he argued, was to balance man's natural character with the refinement of art and education. Confucius believed that "when nature exceeds art you have the rustic. When art exceeds nature you have the clerk. It is only when art and nature are harmoniously blended that you have the gentleman."[14]

An emphasis on self-discipline can have tremendously positive affects on environmentalism. It is the lack of self-discipline—corporate greed, materialism, and unfettered capitalism—that has led to environmental degradation, many would argue. Confucius believed that desires and passions should be kept within an ecologically acceptable limit. Therefore, "Confucius fished, but not with a net; he shot, but not at a perched bird."[15]

Neo-Confucians also emphasized self-discipline. For example, the eleventh-century intellectual Zhang Zai wrote about man's relationship with heaven and earth. Man, he declared, should exercise self-discipline, restraint, and a loving sense of responsibility within his universe. He wrote:

Heaven is my father and earth is my mother, and even such a small creature as I finds an intimate place in their midst.

Therefore that which extends throughout the universe I regard as my body and that which directs the universe I consider my nature.

All people are my brothers and sisters, and all things are my companions....

Wealth, honor, blessing, and benefit are meant for the enrichment of my life, while poverty, humble station, care, and sorrow will be my helpmates to fulfillment.

In life I follow and serve [Heaven and earth]. In death I will be at peace.[16]

Self-discipline, along with self-sacrifice, is a valuable cultural inheritance from Confucianism that can be tremendously helpful in the present-day environmental movement. By sacrificing instant gratification and replacing it with a moral concern for heaven and earth, China's citizens can reverse many of the troubling ecological disasters of the past fifty years, especially those that have emerged as a result of China's headlong rush into capitalism.

Confucianism and Harmony

Closely related to self-discipline, Confucianism has long stressed the necessity for harmonious living. In his own time, Confucius hoped to end the incessant civil wars that were plaguing China and to instill harmony and civility into his world. But Confucius was concerned primarily with social, not ecological harmony. His was clearly an anthropocentric view of the universe. As he reportedly explained, "Man occupies the most honored position in the scheme of things because he combines in him the principles of all species. If he honors his own position and enhances his honor, he can make all species serve him."[17]

This is not to say that Confucius was not concerned for the environment, but that he saw man as different from, and superior to, his physical world. He mocked those who advocated the recluse lifestyle, saying "It is impossible to associate with birds and beasts, as if they were the same with us. If I associate not with these people,—with mankind,—with whom shall I associate?"[18] The *Analects* also record, "When the stables were burned down.., Confucius asked: 'Has any man been hurt?' He did not ask about the horses."[19] Clearly, human victims were more important than animal victims. As the scholar Russell Kirkland pointed out, "The Confucian sage-king is generally one who engenders moral harmony among human beings, not one who inflames sentimental solicitude for oxen, cute puppies, or adorable dolphins."[20]

Despite Confucius' anthropocentrism, subsequent disciples applied his emphasis on harmony to the physical world as well. Writing in the Ming Dynasty, the Neo-Confucian Wang Yang-ming (1472-1529) discussed harmony between man and nature. If motivated by humaneness (or *ren*), the gentleman will seek harmony among humans, animals, plants, and even inanimate natural objects. Wang explained:

> The great man regards Heaven and earth and the myriad things as one body. He regards the world as one family and the country as one person. As to those who make a cleavage between objects and distinguish between the self and others, they are small men. That the great man can regard Heaven, earth, and the myriad things as one body is not because he deliberately wants to do so, but because it is natural with the humane nature of his mind that he should form a unity with Heaven, earth, and the myriad things. This is true not only of the great man. Even the mind of the small man is no different. Only he himself makes it small. Therefore when he sees a child about to fall into a well, he cannot help a feeling of alarm and commiseration. This shows that his humanity (*ren*) forms one body with the child. It may be objected that the child belongs to the same species [as he]. Yet when he observes the pitiful cries and frightened appearance of birds and animals [about to be slaughtered], he cannot help feeling an "inability to bear" their suffering. This shows that his humanity forms one body with birds and animals. It may be objected that birds and animals are sentient beings [as he is]. But when he sees plants broken and destroyed, he cannot help a feeling of pity. This shows that his humanity forms one body with plants. It may be said that plants are living things [as he is]. Yet even when he sees tiles and stones shattered and crushed he cannot help a feeling of regret. This shows that his humanity forms one body with tiles and stones. This means that even the mind of the small man necessarily has the humanity that forms one body with all.[21]

The initial anthropocentrism of Confucianism seems to be an impediment to modern environmentalism. If man is separate from his environment and superior to other living beings, why not dam the Three Gorges? On the other hand, Wang Yangming demonstrated that Confucianism's emphasis on harmony can easily be altered to include harmony between man and nature. Conscious environmentalists can incorporate or ignore those aspects of the Confucian tradition that will best serve their interests.

Confucianism and Activism

Confucius said, "I once spent a whole day without food and a whole night without sleep, in order to meditate. It was no use. It is better to learn."[22] As evidenced in this statement, Confucianism is a doctrine of action, not passivity. Confucius himself used his talents and skills to uplift and enrich his own society.

Like Confucius, Wang Yangming spent his life working to bring about improvements in society. During the Ming Dynasty (1368-1644), Wang had an active career as a statesman and a soldier. In his writings, Wang elaborated on the necessity for action as opposed to inactive, pensive knowledge. He explained:

> There have never been people who know but do not act. Those who are supposed to know but do not act simply do not yet know.... [For example,] seeing beautiful colors appertains to knowledge, while loving beautiful colors appertains to action. However, as soon as one sees a beautiful color, he had already loved it. Smelling a bad odor appertains to knowledge, while hating a bad odor appertains to action. However, as soon as one smells a bad odor, he has already hated it. It is not that he smells it first and then makes up his mind to hate it. A person with his nose stopped up does not smell the dab odor even if he sees a malodorous object before him, and so he does not hate it. This amounts to not knowing bad odor. Suppose we say that so-and-so knows filial piety and so-and-so knows brotherly respect. They must have actually practiced filial piety and brotherly respect before they can be said to know them. It will not do to say that they know filial piety and brotherly respect simply because they show them in words. Or take one's knowledge of pain. Only after one has experienced pain can one know pain. The same is true of cold or hunger. How can knowledge and action be separated? ...I have said that knowledge is the crystallization of the will to act and action is the task of carrying out that knowledge; knowledge is the beginning of action and action is the completion of knowledge.[23]

Confucianism's emphasis on action seems to correlate well with the activism of environmentalists. Most international environmental groups have become effective lobbyists, demonstrators, and advertisers. The same methods have been applied by China's environmentalists. For instance, in a recent crusade, college students, pop singers, Internet chat-room dwellers, and other diverse individuals rallied against the seemingly innocuous chopstick. The production, use, and disposal of 45 billion wooden chopsticks each year, they claim, will wipe out China's remaining forests within a decade. The only solution is to ban disposable chopsticks.[24]

Activists have also targeted the Three Gorges Dam. Many individuals have organized protest marches against the dam.[25] Most of these are individuals whose homes have been relocated away from the flood zone and are not necessarily concerned with the environmental impact of the dam. Nevertheless, they have couched their arguments in persuasive environmental terms.

Activism, however, may also be a liability. One of the primary causes of environmental degradation is the refusal to recognize humanity's interconnectedness with the larger ecology. The belief that man can actively save, restore, or improve the environment seems doomed to fall into the same anthropocentric trap that environmentalists claim to reject. For example, realizing that desertification in western China is one cause of Beijing's annual dust storms, government leaders have decided to create "green belts" surrounding the capital city. By planting concentric circles of trees around Beijing, government officials hope to screen out the flying dust before it afflicts city residents. These green belts will only be the start of the project. The government has pledged an additional $6 billion to plant trees across 250,000 square miles from Beijing to Inner Mongolia.[26] The project has come to be known as the "Green Wall of China."

While the "Green Wall" may sound environmentally friendly and will no doubt help the dust storm situation, it will probably also create unforeseen ecological problems. Environmental activism, however well intentioned, may not necessarily be environmentally friendly.[27] For this reason, it is difficult to assess the long-term value of Confucian-inspired activism for China's environment.

By looking at Confucianism as it relates to self discipline, harmony, and activism, we see that the philosophy has tremendous potential for environmentalists. Though it is not a perfect fit, Confucianism promotes values that can effectively promote environmental conservation. An analysis of Daoism as it relates to these same three areas demonstrates similar challenges and opportunities.

Relevant Teachings of Daoism

According to tradition, Daoism originated from the teachings of Laozi around the time of Confucius. His followers eventually compiled his teaching into the *Dao De Jing*. Though there is debate as to whether Laozi is a mythical or historical figure, the *Dao De Jing* has been immensely influential. The second great Daoist thinker was "Master Zhuang" (Zhuangzi). Master Zhuang lived from 369 to 298 BCE and was probably an intellectual rival of the leading Confucians of that time. Like both Laozi and Confucius, Master Zhuang's disciples collected and edited his teachings and compiled them in a text known simply as the *Zhuangzi*. While the *Dao De Jing* is rather arcane and difficult to understand, the *Zhuangzi* is much more approachable. They are similar, however, in that both analyze and discuss the role and power of the *Dao*.

The *Dao* is difficult to define. Indeed, according to the *Dao De Jing*, "Those who understand do not talk, and those who talk do not understand."[28] Most Daoists define the *Dao* as "a way" or more accurately, "the way." It is the natural way, or the way of the universe. The key to happiness, Daoists might argue, is to live your life in harmony with nature, or the way, rather than constantly fighting against nature or seeking to mold it to your liking. One symbol of Daoism is the un-carved block of wood or stone. Daoists contend that in its natural, unrefined state, the block is more beautiful than anything a skilled craftsman might create from it.

Closely related to this emphasis on the *Dao* is the concept of *wu-wei*. Sometimes translated as inaction, *wu-wei* can be more accurately defined as non-action or, better still, non-striving action. It is only when man strives to change his environment that he upsets the natural order of things. Therefore, a Daoist should not seek to improve his lot in life by studying long hours in school.[29] He should not seek to overcome or alter the restrictions of the physical world. As recorded in the *Zhuangzi*, "In action, stop at what cannot be done. Employ [the faculties] as they would use themselves. Do things that would be done by themselves. Be unrestrained within one's lot but do not attempt the least outside of it. This is the easiest way of taking no [unnatural] action."[30] A true Daoist should not even fight against death, but instead should merely accept it as a natural occurrence. According to the *Zhuangzi*, a certain "Master Yu" fell ill. When his friends arrived to visit him, he exclaimed:

> "Look, the Creator is making me all crookedy! My back sticks up like a hunchback's so that my vital organs are on top of me. My chin is hidden down around my navel, my shoulders are up above my head, and my pigtail points at the sky…"
> "Do you resent it," [asked his friends].
> "Why no," replied Master Yu. "What is there to resent? If the process continues, perhaps in time he'll transform my left arm into a rooster: in that case I'll herald the dawn with my crowing. Or in time he may transform my right arm into a crossbow

> pellet and I'll shoot down an owl for roasting. Or perhaps he will even turn my buttocks into cartwheels: Then with my spirit for a horse, I'll climb up and go for a ride, and never again have need for a carriage.
>
> "I received life because the time had come; I will lose it because the order of things passes on. If only a man will be content with this time and dwell in this order neither sorrow nor joy can touch him."[31]

Just as a Daoist should not seek to alter nature, he should certainly not strive to alter someone else's natural circumstances. In many ways, Daoism is an extremely individualistic philosophy. Early Daoism lacked any organized religious structure or priesthood. Furthermore, early Daoists refused to serve in public office. According to the *Zhuangzi*, once Master Zhuang was fishing when two ministers approached him and asked him to serve as an official for the King of Chu. Without turning his head, Zhuangzi replied:

> "I have heard that in Chu there is a spirit-like tortoise-shell, the wearer of which died 3,000 years ago, and which the king keeps, in his ancestral temple, in a hamper covered with a cloth. Was it better for the tortoise to die, and leave its shell to be thus honoured? Or would it have been better for it to live, and keep on dragging its tail through the mud?"
>
> The two officers said, "It would have been better for it to live, and draw its tail after it over the mud."
>
> "Go your ways, [Zhuangzi replied.] I will keep on drawing my tail after me through the mud."[32]

After the Han emperors declared Confucianism the state philosophy (during the second century BCE), Daoism waned in influence. Within three hundred years, Daoism had been largely subsumed within Confucianism and folk religion. Following the collapse of the Han, however, Daoism's fortunes changed. Intellectuals that had previously focused on Confucianism rediscovered the Daoist classics, sparking a revival in commentaries on the *Dao De Jing* and the *Zhuangzi*. These intellectuals, including Wang Bi (226-249 CE) and Guo Xiang (d. 312 CE), sought to integrate Daoism and Confucianism to better understand each. By the fourth century CE, Daoism, or "Neo-Daoism," had experienced a tremendous revival.

It was not only secular intellectuals that rediscovered Daoism at this time. Religious reformers also turned increasingly toward this school of thought for answers. In an unusual twist, Daoism became identified with the search for immortality. Daoist practitioners included many of the best alchemists, each seeking a concoction that would bring him eternal life. At the same time, Daoism incorporated and codified many folk religious practices. By the sixth century, Daoism was declared the state religion. Though Daoists of this period still revered the *Dao De Jing* and the *Zhuangzi*, their philosophies had changed dramatically.

From the ninth century on, Daoism again waned in influence. Imperial rulers believed Confucianism was a more appropriate doctrine for governing, and Daoism lost its official patronage. Nevertheless, Daoist philosophy and ideas remained immensely influential in art, literature, and religion.

Daoism and Self-Discipline

As with Confucianism, self-control and self-discipline are primary concerns for the Daoist. There are numerous selections from the *Dao De Jing* and the *Zhuangzi* to support this contention. The *Dao De Jing* writes that if man would quit seeking profit and accumulating wealth, thieves and robbers would disappear. Instead, man should "diminish [his] selfishness and reduce [his] desires" and "be as pure as undyed silk and as simple as uncarved wood."[33] If there were a state completely populated with such people, the *Dao De Jing* teaches:

> Though [the residents] had boats and carriages, they should have no occasion to ride in them; though they had buff coats and sharp weapons, they should have no occasion to don or use them.... They [would] think their (course) food sweet; their (plain) clothes beautiful; their (poor) dwellings places of rest; and their common (simple) ways sources of enjoyment.[34]

Though these sections suggest that Daoism, contentment, and self-restraint are coterminous, Daoism certainly should not be confused with asceticism or self-denial. Some, including many Confucians, have argued that Daoism actually promotes self-indulgence and egocentrism. There have been numerous historical examples of self-indulgent Daoists. One of these, Yang Zhu, has often been portrayed as a hedonist. Describing his carefree and pleasure-seeking attitude toward life, Yang wrote:

> Half of [a man's life] is occupied with infancy and senility. Of the other half, almost half is wasted in sleep at night and naps in the day time. And almost half of the remainder is lost in pain, illness, sorrow, grief, death, and loss [of relatives and friends]. I would estimate that in the ten years or more [that is left to him] a man has hardly one hour in which he is quite content and free from the slightest worry. Then what is the purpose of life? What is the joy of life? Life is only for [the enjoyment of] beauty and wealth, and sound and color. But beauty and wealth cannot always be enjoyed to satisfaction, and color and sound cannot always be indulged in. Instead, we are forbidden by penalties from doing this and are exhorted by rewards to do that.... Thus we do but miss the perfect happiness of the years as they go by, and cannot give ourselves free rein even for an hour. What is the difference between this and being doubly chained inside an inner prison...? Let us enjoy this life. Why be concerned with the hereafter?[35]

According to these passages, it appears that classical Daoism has elements of both self-denial as well as self-gratification. Neo-Daoism also has these same two characteristics. In their quest for immortality, Neo-Daoists believed that a man needed a perfect balance of the elements *yin* and *yang*.[36] Since the *yin* element was associated with femaleness and the *yang* element was associated with maleness, Neo-Daoists alleged that during sexual relations, a man should capture the *yin* of the woman without losing any of his own *yang*. While these sexual practices might be interpreted as a sign of self denial (at least for the male practitioners), literature suggests that sex was extremely pleasurable for the Neo-Daoists.[37] Furthermore, Daoist sexual relations were not limited to monogamous couples but transgressed many of the social mores advocated by the more puritanical Confucians.

What, then, are Daoism's ramifications for modern environmentalism? Depending on your interpretation and historical examples, Daoism is a philosophy that emphasizes both self-restraint as well as self-indulgence. A modern-day Daoist might argue that driving an uneconomical luxury automobile is perfectly acceptable, as long as the vehicle brings carefree happiness to its owner.[38] On the other hand, a Daoist might argue that such a vehicle is an "ill-provided adornment of life" and that its owner would do better to "see the simple, embrace primitivity…reduce the self, [and] lessen the desires."[39] Environmentalists will need to emphasize the latter while ignoring the former to achieve success in contemporary China.

Daoism and Harmony

In Western popular culture, Confucians are often portrayed as aspiring artificers seeking social harmony at the expense of individual freedom while having little concern for their natural world. Daoists, on the other hand, are portrayed as liberated, unconventional, maverick loners that are more comfortable in a forest than in a crowded room. According to these stereotypes, social harmony is not a primary concern of the Daoist.

However, it appears as if Daoism is intensely concerned about living a life in harmony with nature. As mentioned earlier, Daoism emphasizes the un-carved block, or the block that is in harmony with the *Dao* and its natural state. Only when man is living in harmony with the *Dao*, or nature, can he be truly carefree and content. Furthermore, if all men were living in harmony with nature, social harmony would be the unintended byproduct.

Daoism's emphasis on nature can be best appreciated through a study of art. During the early centuries CE, Daoists were renowned for their *shan-shui* paintings (meaning "mountain-river paintings" or more simply "landscape paintings"). These paintings, which depict the beautiful topography of southern China, are not accurate, three-dimensional representations of the environment. Instead, the artists intended to visually represent the *Dao* of the natural world, emphasizing man's harmony with the *Dao*. Consequently, the mist-shrouded mountains of these paintings oftentimes have very small human figures in the foreground—part of the picture, but only a very small and non-central part. Instead, the images lift the viewer's eyes upward toward the peaks of the stylized mountains.[40]

Depicting man's relationship to nature, the fifth-century Daoist painter Zong Bing explained:

> As to landscapes, they exist in material substance and soar into the realm of the spirit.… Now the sage, by the exercise of his spirit, follows Dao as his standard, while the worthy man understands this. Mountains and rivers in their form pay homage to Dao, and the man of humanity delights in them. Do not the sage and mountains and rivers have much in common?[41]

Because of its emphasis on living in harmony with nature, it is easy to see why many environmental activists have been drawn toward Daoism. Indeed, if more individuals had a healthy, Daoist respect for the natural world, many of our modern environmental woes would be eliminated. Ironically, many of those who value Daoism for its environmental benefits live outside of China. For instance, the Britain-based Taoist Cultural Arts Association explains in their mission proposal statement:

> [We propose] to initiate a sustainable countryside development project…based around the theme of living in balance with the natural environment. We will provide a range of other activities including accommodation, Arts and Craft workshops and a variety of ongoing projects to showcase the latest developments in sustainable countryside development, organic farming techniques, renewable energy and alternative technology.[42]

It remains to be seen if environmental groups can generate the same type of enthusiasm toward environmental Daoism within China.

Daoism and Activism

As discussed earlier, Daoism teaches that man should not seek to alter the *Dao*. "Do not let the artificial obliterate the natural; do not let effort obliterate destiny," the *Zhuangzi* teaches.[43] Instead, man should emphasize *wu-wei*, or non-striving action. Perhaps more than any other Daoist teaching, the concept of *wu-wei* has tremendous implications for modern environmentalism. If man were to follow the *Dao* and refrain from acting contrary to "the way," it would seem that many of our environmental problems would disappear.

The Three Gorges Dam provides an excellent case study for the concept of *wu-wei*. As the Daoist classics teach, water is the ultimate symbol of non-striving action. Water always follows the course of least resistance—it always follows "the way." Just as a small stream gently wends its way around an imposing rock, so too should the Daoist follow the path of least resistance. By blocking the natural flow of the river, the builders of the Three Gorges Dam are violating "the way." The immediate result will be flooding, the destruction of ecologies, and the obliteration of millions of acres of natural wildlife.

There is, however, an alternate prediction for the Three Gorges Dam. To return to the river-and-rock analogy, though the river flows around the rock, eventually the water will polish the rock into a smooth river stone. Over an even longer period of time, the stone will be worn down to a small pebble and eventually will be washed away with the spring floods. Through non-striving action, the water accomplishes tremendous feats. It would seem the long term prognosis for the Three Gorges Dam is not good.

Just as Master Yu did not fight death, but instead rejoiced as his "buttocks became cartwheels," the environmental Daoist should not seek to prevent nature from running its course. But who is to say what that natural course is? Are the actions of the dam builders inappropriate, or are the actions of the dam protestors inappropriate? The simple Daoist answer is that they both are ignoring the concept of *wu-wei* and therefore are equally blameworthy. Activism, even environmental activism, is contrary to Daoist teachings. When an activist protests the building of a dam, the polluting of a river, or the destruction of a rain forest, he is arrogantly suggesting that he best understands (and controls) "the way." As Russell Kirkland explains in *Daoism and Ecology*, "from the classical Daoist perspective, it is clearly morally suspect for humans to presume that they are justified in judging what might constitute 'impending ecological danger…' The classical Daoist position is that planet Earth needs no savior as such, especially not ourselves."[44]

Because of the differing implications for *wu-wei*, environmental activists must be selective in using and applying Daoist teachings to modern problems. The idea of non-action certainly sounds pro-environment, yet non-action also precludes activism. As they argue that dam builders and other enemies of the environment are acting in ways contrary to the *Dao*, so too can they find the same argument reapplied to their own environmental actions.

Conclusion

China's environmentalists have found that they must use a variety of approaches as they advocate for cleaner water, resource preservation, and the protection of endangered species. At times, protests and demonstrations have brought about changes in environmental policy. At other times, conciliation and cooperation have been more effective.[45] Depending on the particulars of the situation, environmentalists can appeal to such values as self discipline, harmony with nature, and appropriate activism (and in-activism). Fortunately, each of these has roots in China's religious and philosophical past. In their own ways, both Confucianism and Daoism have much to offer to China's current environmentalists.

When it is completed, the Three Gorges Dam will be 600 feet high, one and a half miles wide, and will create a reservoir nearly 400 miles long. Dam planners expect it will reduce flooding in the region, provide hydroelectric power to millions of homes and businesses, and allow ocean freighters to travel deep into the interior of the nation. It will be, some hope, a panacea for many of China's existing problems.

Others, however, are not so optimistic. Dai Qing, a trained scientist and investigative journalist, has been one of the most outspoken critics of the dam. Calling it "the most environmentally and socially destructive project in the world," Dai was imprisoned by government authorities for challenging their leadership in the plan.[46] Her imprisonment did not silence her. After migrating to the United States, Dai compiled a collection of essays critical of the dam and continued to be one of its leading opponents.[47]

Despite its sometimes heavy-handed tactics, the government is listening to Dai and others like her. In February 2005, China's State Environmental Protection Agency (SEPA) ordered a temporary halt to the construction of the dam. The construction company, according to SEPA, had failed to file the proper environmental statements. SEPA allowed the developer extra time to submit the necessary paperwork, but warned that if it failed to do so, it would impose a fine of Rmb 200,000 (roughly US$24,000).[48] While such an amount is pitifully small, it represents SEPA's growing authority and credibility. Environmentalists have witnessed many such small but noticeable changes in Chinese society and they will no doubt continue to influence business, government, and economic development in the future.[49]

For many, such changes are not significant enough. China's skies and rivers are still the most polluted in the world, and the situation will probably get worse, at least in the short term. As the Chinese plod through the quagmires of industrialization, they are simultaneously dealing with the environmental side-effects that come with that process. Fortunately, many of the answers to those problems can be found in their own intellectual past.

Notes

1. See, for example, D. Moore, *Zen Gardening Kit* (Running Press Books, 1992); Jenny Hendy, *Zen in Your Garden: Creating Sacred Spaces* (Charles E. Tuttle Co., Inc, 2001); Pamela K. Metz, *The Tao of Gardening: A Collection of Reflections Adapted from Lao Tzu's Tao Te Ching* (Humanics Trade, 2001); Gill Hale and Sue Minter, *Feng Shui Garden: Design Your Garden for Health, Wealth and Happiness* (Storey Books, 1998); Raymond Olson, *Blending with Nature: Classical Chinese Gardens in the Suzhou Style* (Vancouver, WA: Sacred Mountain Productions, 2003)—a video.
2. "China emerges as global consumer," *BBC News*, 17 February 2005 (http://news.bbc.co.uk/1/hi/world/asia-pacific/4272577.stm, (last accessed 8 June 2005).
3. Michael Mackey, "Fuel cells may fuel a cleaner China," Asia Times, 26 June 2004 (http://www.atimes.com/atimes/China/FF26Ad06.html, (last accessed 8 June 2005).
4. See, for example, Judith Shapiro, *Mao's War Against Nature: Politics and the Environment in Revolutionary China* (Cambridge: Cambridge University Press, 2001).
5. Tong Wu, "Three Gorges: The Price of Progress," *Asia Times*, 16 August 2003, http://www.atimes.com/atimes/China/EH16Ad01.html (last accessed 8 June 2005).
6. Andrew Yeh, "China orders halt to part of Three Gorges dam," Financial Times, 2 February 2005. Available online at http://yaleglobal.yale.edu/display.article?id=3250 (last accessed 2 February 2005).
7. As Peter Ho and Richard Louis Edmonds point out, environmental activists are on the cutting edge of China's emerging civil society. However, due to the political context, China's environmental movement is decentralized and fragmented. "Chinese green activists," Ho and Edmonds point out, "[keep] a safe distance from direct political action." See Peter Ho and Richard Louis Edmonds, "Environmentalism and Civil Society," *International Institute for Asian Studies Newsletter*, 37 (July 2005): 9. See also Peter Ho, "Greening without Conflict? Environmentalism, Green NGOs and Civil Society in China," *Development and Change*, 32 (2001): 893-921.
8. For an understanding of China's environmental problems and some of the steps being taken to ameliorate these problems, see Deirdre Chetham, *Before the Deluge: The Vanishing world of the Yangtze's Three Gorges* (New York: Palgrave Macmillan, 2002); Richard Louis Edmonds, ed., *Managing the Chinese Environment* (Oxford: Oxford University Press, 2000); Elizabeth C. Economy, *The River Runs Black: The Environmental Challenge to China's Future* (Ithaca, NY: Cornell University Press, 2004).
9. These conferences took place between 1996 and 1998. For more information about the meetings and participants, or for a listing of presentation abstracts, see the website "Religions of the World and Ecology" sponsored by the Harvard Divinity School available at http://www.hds.harvard.edu/cswr/research/ecology/index.html (last accessed 18 March 2005).
10. Mary Evelyn Tucker and Duncan Ryken Williams, eds., *Buddhism and Ecology: The Interconnection of Dharma and Deeds* (Cambridge, MA: Harvard University Press, 1997); Mary Evelyn Tucker and John Berthrong, eds., *Confucianism and Ecology: The Interrelation of Heaven, Earth, and Humans* (Cambridge, MA: Harvard University Press, 1998); N.J. Girardot, James Miller, and Liu Xiaogan, eds., *Daoism and Ecology: Ways within a Cosmic Landscape* (Cambridge, MA: Harvard University Press, 2001).

    Though not a part of the above conference, another interesting work that looks at the impact of eastern religions on the environmental movement is David E. Cooper and Simon P. James, *Buddhism, Virtue and Environment* (Burlington, VT: Ashgate, 2005). This text argues that Buddhism is primarily a social, not an environmental philosophy. Nevertheless, its teaching can be selectively applied to environmental movements. The text does not look specifically at China's environmental movement. See also Simon P. James, *Zen Buddhism and Environmental Ethics* (Burlington, VT: Ashgate, 2004).
11. As this essay will show, both Confucianism and Daoism are complex philosophies that advocate conflicting ideas. Furthermore, these philosophies have changed dramatically over the past two millennia. The purpose of this paper is not to demonstrate that one school of thought is inherently more environmentally logical or appropriate. Instead, I will highlight some of the teachings and beliefs of these philosophies that can either be *selectively* used or ignored by environmentalists in China today.
12. Fan Zhongyan as quoted by Charles O. Hucker, *China's Imperial Past* (Stanford, CA: Stanford University Press, 1975), 364.

13. *The Confucian Analects*, Book XVII, Chapter 2. Translation by William Theodore deBary, Wing-Tsit Chan, and Burton Watson, comps., *Sources of Chinese Tradition*, vol. 1 (New York: Columbia University Press, 1960), 23.

    There are many versions of the *Analects* available in Chinese and in English translations. For this paper, I used the volume *Confucius: Confucian Analects, The Great Learning, and The Doctrine of the Mean* (New York: Dover Publications, 1971) which contains both the Chinese as well as English translations by James Legge. In Legge's work, the original book and chapter organization has been maintained. Therefore, in this and subsequent citations, I simply refer to the book and chapter of the *Analects*. I also specify which translation of the *Analects* I am using.
14. *The Analects*, VI:16; translation by deBary, Chan, and Watson, 30.
15. *The Analects*, VII:26; This translation is my own.
16. Zhang Zhai, *Zhang hengju ji*, I:1a-5b as quoted in deBary, Chan, and Watson, 469-70.
17. *Huangji jingshi shu*, 7A:4a-8b:26a as quoted in deBary, Chan, and Watson, 463-64.
18. *The Analects*, XVIII:6; translation by Legge, *Confucius*, 334.
19. *The Analects* X:12; translation my own.
20. Russell Kirkland, "'Responsible Non-Action' in a Natural World: Perspectives from the *Neiye, Zhuangzi*, and *Daode jing*," *Daoism and Ecology*, 304.
21. Wang Yangmin, *Yangming quanshu*, 26:1b-5a as quoted by deBary, Chan, and Watson, 516-517.
22. *The Analects* XV:30; Translation by Arthur Waley, trans., *The Analects of Confucius* (London: George Allen and Unwin, Ltd., 1964), 199.
23. Wang Yangmin, *Yangming quanshu*, I:3ab as quoted by deBary, Chan, and Watson, 524.
24. Philip P. Pan, "China's Chopsticks Crusade: Drive Against Disposables Feeds Environmental Movement," Washington Post, 6 February 2001, pg. A01. Available online at: http://washingtonpost.com/wp-dyn/world/asia/A3296-2001Jan30.html (last accessed 6 March 2001).
25. Jasper Becker, "China awakens to its devastated environment," Asia Times Online, 29 August 2003. Available online at http://www.atimes.com/atimes/China/EH29Ad01.html (last accessed 18 March 2005).
26. Robert Marquand, "Beijing fends off monsters on its steppes," Christian Science Monitor, 22 March 2002. Available online at http://www.csmonitor.com/2002/0322/p07s01-woap.html (last accessed 18 March 2005).
27. There are numerous such examples of well-intentioned activism that have proven to be controversial or even disastrous. One is the case of seal hunting in Canada. When anti-sealing campaigns in the early 1980s led to declining revenues for seal pelts, Inuit seal-hunting societies suffered tremendously, leading to increased suicide rates, increased welfare rates, and the loss of economic independence. Another such case from roughly the same time period involved the U.S. Forest Service and its decision to allow Yellowstone to burn with forest fires. See, Alston Chase, *Playing God in Yellowstone: The Destruction of America's First National Park* (Boston: Atlantic Monthly Press, 1986).
28. *The Daode Jing*, chapter 1, translation by Hucker, 89.

    There are many versions of both the *Daode Jing* and *The Zhuangzi*. For this paper, I used Legge's translations titled *The Texts of Taoism* and Wang Rongpei and William Puffenberger translation titled, *Tao Te Ching* (Lianing, China: Liaoning University Press, 1996). Wang and Puffenberger's volume contains both the Chinese as well as English translations. In this and subsequent citations, I simply refer to the book and chapter of either *The Daode Jing* or *The Zhuangzi*. I also specify which translation I am using.
29. Related to this de-emphasis of education, Daoists also belittled those that engaged in endless philosophical debates. *The Zhuangzi* is a text of fantasy and skepticism rather than a persuasive, argumentative text. For example, *The Zhuangzi* writes, "the scintillations of light from the midst of confusion and perplexity are indeed valued by the sagely man; but not to use one's own views and to take his position on the ordinary views is what is called using the (proper) light.... But though this be the case, let me try to explain myself. There was a beginning. There was beginning before that beginning. There was a beginning previous to that beginning before there was the beginning. There was existence; there had been no existence. There was no existence before the beginning of that no existence. There was no existence previous to the no existence before there was the beginning of the no existence. If suddenly there was non-existence, we do not know whether it was really anything existing, or really not existing. Now I have said what I have said, but I do not know whether what I have said be really anything to the point or not." *The Zhaungzi*, Book 2, Part 1, Section 3. Translation by James Legge, *The Texts of Taoism* (New York: Dover Publications, 1962), 187.

30. Guo Xiang, *Commentary of The Zhuangzi* as quoted in deBary, Chan, and Watson, 245.
31. *The Zhuangzi* Book 6, Part 1, Section 6, translated by Burton Watson, *Chuang Tzu: Basic Writings* (New York: Columbia University Press, 1996).
32. *The Zhuangzi*, Book 17, Part 2, Section 10, translated by Legge, *The Texts of Taoism* 390.
33. *Dao De Jing*, chapter 19, translated by Wang and Puffenberger, 49.
34. *Dao De Jing*, Chapter 80, translated by Legge, *The Texts of Taoism*, 122.
35. Yang Zhu, *Lie Zi*, 7:1b-2a as quoted by deBary, Chan, and Watson, 250-251.
36. The *International Encyclopedia of Sexuality* explains, "According to the Yin-Yang philosophy, all objects and events are the products of two elements, forces, or principles: Yin, which is negative, passive, weak, and destructive; and Yang, which is positive, active, strong, and constructive. It was very natural for the Yin-Yang doctrine to become the basis of Chinese sexual philosophy. The Chinese have used the words Yin and Yang to refer to sexual organs and sexual behavior for several thousand years. Thus *Yin Fu,* "the door of Yin" means vulva, *Yin Dao,* "the passageway of Yin" means vagina, and *Yang Ju,* "the organ of Yang" means penis. The combination of these words into the phrases *Huo Yin Yang or Yin Yang Huo He* – "the union or combination of Yin and Yang" – describes the act of sexual intercourse." See Fang Furuan and M.P. Lau, "China (Zhonghua Renmin Gonghe Guo)," *The International Encyclopedia of Sexuality*, Robert T. Francour, ed. (New York: Continuum Publishing Company, 2003), reproduced online at http://www2.hu-berlin.de/sexology/IES/ (last accessed 22 August 2005).
37. Jacob Pastoetter, "Vietnam (*Công Hoa Xa Hôi Chú Nghia Viêt Nam*) Socialist Republic of Vietnam," *The International Encyclopedia of Sexuality.*
38. Despite the existence of massive traffic jams and the lack of parking space, Chinese sales of sport utility vehicles (SUVs) have skyrocketed in recent years. During the summer of 2004, I saw a dealership in downtown Beijing selling the massively self-indulgent "Hummer" vehicle. According to "Autoblog," sales of SUVs in China increased over 200 percent between 2001 and 2003. As such, SUVs represent the fastest growing segment of the Chinese auto market. See http://www.autoblog.com/entry/0535432654354065/ (last accessed 5 June 2005).
39. *Dao De Jing*, chapter 19, translated by deBary, Chan, and Watson, 55.
40. Such art forms remained popular right up into the twentieth century. After the communist revolution, however, social realism became the dominant art form in China. As with traditional *shan-shui* paintings, the art of the early communist period also portrayed mountains, rivers, and forests. Unlike the Daoist versions, these paintings included large, muscular human figures placed dominantly in the foreground and flanked not only by mountains, but also by electricity poles, dams, and smoke-belching tractors. In other words, the art of this period actively portrayed Mao Zedong's "war against nature."
41. Zong Bing, *Lidai minghua ji*, 6:3b-4b, translated by deBary, Chan, and Watson, 253.
42. Taoist Cultural Arts Association website, http://www.seahorsearts.co.uk/taichicentre.htm (last accessed 21 June 2005).
43. *The Zhuangzi*, Book 17, Part 2, Section 10, translated by deBary, Chan, and Watson 77.
44. Kirkland 289.
45. See Ho and Edmonds, "Environmentalism and Civil Society"; Ho, "Greening without Conflict? Environmentalism, Green NGOs and Civil Society in China"; and Yiyi Lu, "Civil society groups rely on Beijing." Asia Times Online, 5 May 2005, http://www.atimes.com/atimes/China/GE05Ad02.html (last accessed 9 September 2005).
46. Bruce Kennedy, "China's Three Gorges Dam," *CNN.com* special series titled "Visions of China: 50 Years of the People's Republic," October 1999, http://www.cnn.com/specials/1999/china.50/asian.superpower/three.gorges/ (last accessed 21 June 2005).
47. Dai Qing, ed., *The River Dragon Has Come!: The Three Gorges Dam and the Fate of China's Yangtze River and Its People* (Armonk, NY: M. E. Sharpe, 1997).
48. Andrew Yeh, "China orders halt to part of Three Gorges Dam," *The Financial Times*, 2 February 2005, http://news.ft.com/cms/s/c487b666-750a-11d9-9608-00000e2511c8.html (last accessed 15 March 2005).
49. There have been numerous such "victories" in China during the past several months. For a look at other, recent environmental changes, see Lu, "Civil society groups rely on Beijing" **and** "Violent protests at Chinese plant," CNN.com, 22 August 2005, http://www.cnn.com/2005/WORLD/asiapcf/08/22/china.stability.reut/index.html (last accessed 9 September 2005).

Frontier and Virgin: The Historical Landscapes of Frederick Jackson Turner and Henry Adams

David S. Brown

In 1895, University of Wisconsin historian Frederick Jackson Turner and former Harvard historian Henry Adams were invited to contribute essays to the inaugural edition of the *American Historical Review*, the flagship publication of the American Historical Association. Beyond their scholarly credentials, peers recognized both men as representatives of distinct sections – Adams the patrician East, Turner the democratic West. *Review* editor John Franklin Jameson explained to Turner the regional implications of his request: "We wish to make [the *Review*] obviously and from the first, an organ representative of the historical scholarship of all sections of the country alike. It is deemed essential that the first numbers...shall contain an article by a representative historical scholar of the West, and, if he is willing, upon some topic of Western history or connected therewith."[1] Accordingly, Turner appeared in the first edition of the *Review*, as did Adams. From that point on, their professional fortunes diverged widely. Turner, despite publishing little, became the most celebrated historian of his generation while the more prolific Adams exerted comparatively little influence on the historical profession.

Coupling Turner and Adams calls upon the careful reader to compare their chief contributions to American historical writing—the frontier and the Virgin. Turner's 1893 essay "The Significance of the Frontier in American History" argued that the act of pioneering encouraged certain qualities—individualism, egalitarianism, pragmatism, and idealism—that broke from hierarchical European practices to produce a uniquely democratic civilization in America. The essay is to this day regularly discussed and debated in colleges and universities. Adams, by comparison, insisted in two notable books, *Mont Saint Michel and Chartres* (1904) and *The Education of Henry Adams* (1907), that reverence for the Virgin Mary both harmonized and humanized Western civilization. Under the inspiration of the Cross, elaborate cathedrals were constructed, European armies fought crusades, and feudal peasants lived under a system of society and economics that was more paternal and less exploitative than the proletariat capitalism of the twentieth century.

As grand historical theories, the frontier and the Virgin would appear to have little in common. The Virgin addressed European history, cherished the undemocratic late Middle Ages, prized the Catholic Church for preserving a priceless culture, and stressed the virtue of a static social order attuned to the casual rhythms of Medieval time, work and leisure. In a Protestant, democratic, capitalist country, Adams's work could not hope to receive the same sunny reception as Turner's. His frontier addressed American history, cherished the democratic Age of Jackson, it prized the wilderness as a heroic landscape that forged a new culture, and stressed the virtue of movement and change in a nation of perpetual pioneers. "As you know," Turner wrote to his last student, the talented University of Wisconsin historian Merle Curti, "the 'West' with which I dealt was a *process* rather than a fixed geographical region.... In short, the 'frontier' was taken as the 'thin red line' that recorded the *dynamic* element in American history."[2]

In sum, Turner's frontier thesis eclipsed Adams's Virgin in the American imagination because it was both more familiar and more useful. Its acceptance among professional historians, however, was not immediate. Antiquarianism dominated the early days of the American Historical Association, and long, dull, and lightly researched papers on battles and local history by non-academics mocked the high scholastic aspirations of the Association's annual meetings. In its first generation of existence, perhaps only a quarter of AHA membership derived from college and university instructors—and many of these men resided in the Midwest, an area then considered very much deficient of serious scholarship. Writing to his father in 1889, Jameson, then a young Brown University professor, criticized the quality of historical activity in America, and confessed further his low opinion of frontier history.

> The candid statement of fact is that the [recent] meetings of the American Historical Association were extremely stupid. The meeting, you remember, was to have occurred at Columbus in September, and the result was, that we had much Western history warmed-over from then. Western history is stupid anyway, I think, and now that the Ohio centennials are over, it all seemed to have a castanean [old-fashioned] flavor as it were.... The men whom I always find most interesting, were almost entirely absent; and of the New England historical professors, most interesting men, only one was present besides me.[3]

Jameson's letter touched upon a number of issues that shaped the AHA in its infancy: the quest for control over historical writing by professionals, the East's disregard for western historiography, and frustration that the scholarship produced by academics had yet to shake the grip of the patricians. In a word, the profession craved legitimacy.

It was, therefore, ironic that the first great idea to secure the reputation of professional historians came from the West. Turner's frontier thesis shattered the eastern historical consensus, validated academic history, and forced men like Jameson to recognize the centrality of western lands, economies, and peoples in American life. It was a role that the AHA had long ignored. In its first twenty years of existence, the Association held its annual conference West of the Alleghenies on only five occasions. The Association's presidency was even more firmly in the hands of eastern men. Between 1884 and 1909, every AHA president (including Adams in 1894) had either been born in the East, or in the cases of Ohio native James Ford Rhodes (1899) and Edward Eggleston of Indiana (1900), had been living there for several years when they were selected Association President. When Turner became president in 1910, he was the first historian in the history of the AHA to be affiliated with a western university —the University of Wisconsin—the year he gave his address.

Turner's thesis offered a new way of looking at the past that placed the Ohio Valley firmly in the center of the American story. More personally, it raised the status and self-esteem of midwestern scholars taught by painful experience to view their professional positions as inferior to their academic brethren in the East. Turner had observed the arrogance of the Brahmins first hand. Harvard President Charles W. Eliot visited the University of Wisconsin in 1891, dismissing at every opportunity Turner's and fellow Madison historian Charles Homer Haskins's Johns Hopkins PhDs. "Didn't we know that Harvard was the place to study history, that they alone had the libraries and the instructors?" Haskins remembered of the inquisition. "It passed [Eliot's] power of comprehension that students in the West were so ignorant of the proper place to pursue graduate studies. He was quite discourteous in his manner and apparently created quite a reaction. Even in the West one is supposed to be a gentleman."[4]

Respect from eastern men like Eliot could be earned only by producing widely acclaimed ideas, essays, and books. Turner succeeded by arguing persuasively that democracy and geography shared a relationship much closer than historians had previously imagined—and that this relationship explained the nation's egalitarian institutions. He made his case less as a conventional historian than as a cutting-edge social scientist, appealing to statistics, census data, and the work of the distinguished Italian economist Achille Loria. Despite its claims of methodological completeness, however, the new history did not please everyone. In his AHA presidential address, delivered the year Turner's frontier thesis was published, Adams complained that American historians were too eager to turn history from an art – reflected in his own conception of the Virgin—into a science. "You may be sure," he insisted, "that four out of five serious students of history who are living today have in the course of their work felt that they stood on the brink of a great generalization that would reduce all history under a law as clear as the laws which govern the material world." "We cannot help asking ourselves," he continued, "what would happen if some new Darwin were to demonstrate the laws of historical evolution."[5]

Certainly Turner conceived of history as a branch of science, and frequently linked his work with Darwin's. The language in his 1896 essay "The Problem of the West" is striking: "The history of our political institutions, our democracy, is. . . a history of the evolution and adaptation of organs in response to changed environment, a history of the origin of new political species."[6] Had Turner's frontier essays merely asserted the particular virtues of pioneer life, his work would quickly have been forgotten. By combining, however, his personal views on democracy, environment, and region to a scientific theory that intellectuals in the East respected he guaranteed its success.

But was Turner's frontier thesis as scientific as he imagined? And was the frontier really the antithesis of Adams's Virgin? As theories of separate eastern and midwestern historical imaginations, it is remarkable how similar they in fact are. In the case of both men, defining childhood episodes forged life-long enthusiasm for the past. The frontier was a living organism to Turner, a real place with vivid sounds and smells. He knew the backwoods from personal experience and recalled with affection his initial immersions into the wilderness. "I remember," he wrote late in life, "when with my father I took one of the first trains through the woods of northern Wisconsin to Lake Superior—a narrow aisle cut like a gash through the wonderful white pine forest. And I remembered a voyage down the Wisconsin, poled by Indians in a dug out from near Wausau, and hearing a duet-like conversation between the boatmen and their squaws as we passed their Indian village—the gutteral of the buck and the sweet, clear, laughing treble of the squaw. I remember the antlered deer who stood at a bend among the balsam firs, drinking at the river's edge, and how close we got to see him in our silent canoe before he snorted and broke for cover."[7]

Adams's early historical references were more melancholy. He watched as the dynamic forces of capitalism and technology destroyed the simple republic created by his ancestors. "For him alone," he wrote of his childhood, "the old universe was thrown into the ash-heap and a new one created. He and his eighteenth-century, troglodytic Boston were suddenly cut apart—separated forever—in act if not in sentiment, by the opening of the Boston and Albany Railroad; the appearance of the first Cunard Steamers in the bay; and the telegraphic messages which carried from Baltimore to Washington the news that Henry Clay and James K. Polk were nominated for the presidency. This was in May, 1844; he was six years old."[8]

Both Turner and Adams recalled eventful pasts in forests and cities that informed their work. Turner portrayed the frontier as a conservatory of enduring democratic values that he hoped might survive the closing of the pioneer phase of American development. His frontier was innocence unspoiled. Adams's Virgin, by contrast, was innocence lost. They agreed, however, on the essential arcadian nature of Europe and America at their best, and respected the anti-modern underpinnings—agrarianism, racial homogeneity, and the absence of large cities—that strengthened those civilizations. They further shared a fascination with the idea of decline. Turner's frontier address responded to the 1890 census's declaration that the free lands were gone. Their demise seemed to anticipate the dominance of the industrial East. Adams too reacted sharply to the peoples of the "East." He referred to the Byzantine Empire and the Moslem Caliphate rather than the American Robber Baron and his immigrant laborers, yet in either context the metaphor of western tradition giving way to eastern change is present. "The East was the common enemy," Adams wrote, "always superior in wealth and numbers, frequently in energy, and sometimes in art and thought."[9]

In response to their disenchantment, with the "new," Turner and Adams developed theories of history that worshiped conventional archetypes—the pioneer, the backwoodsman, and the trapper in Turner's case; the universality of the Cross in Adams's. They moreover led lives that celebrated the subjects of their work. Turner spent many of his adult summers fishing and hiking in Wisconsin and Maine—he clearly loved the outdoors and felt a strong connection to the Midwest's first settlers. Adams traveled extensively in Europe, lovingly studying Medieval architecture, literature, and material cultural. Standing on the rock of Mont Saint Michel in northern France, he embraced the natural environment. Sand, ocean, and sky converged to prepare the pilgrim for his audience with the past. "One must," he wrote of history, "learn to feel it."[10]

The frontier and Virgin shared not only common origins but common enemies. The emergence of an urban, industrial America troubled both Turner and Adams, for the social values of the new order threatened the individualism prized by the former and the cultural accord stressed by the latter. A genteel anti-Semitism underlined their anxieties. In 1887, Turner traveled to Boston for the first time and marveled at the alienness of the city's Jewish section. "Hardly had I turned aside from the noise of Hanover Street when an entirely different atmosphere was entered. The word is well chosen. In a moment I saw what had happened. I was in Jewry, the street consecrated to 'old clothes' pawn brokers, and similar followers of Abraham. It was a narrow *alley*, we would say in the west—and was fairly packed with swarthy sons and daughters of the tribe of Israel—such noises, such smells, such sights....At last, after much elbowing, I came upon the Old North [Church] rising out of this mass of Oriental noise and squalor like a haven or rest."[11]

Some years later, Adams reflected on the meaning of New York City as the world metropolis of "the new forces" that were tearing old America apart. His language—"frantic," "hysteria," "crying," "anger and alarm"—drew a brutal and unsympathetic portrait of the post immigrant city. Like Turner, he looked to the past to explain the present, and appealed to the law of evolution to carry his argument. He broke from Turner, however, by describing American history as a case study of decline—devolution. "A traveler in the highways of history looked out of the club window on the turmoil of Fifth Avenue," he wrote, "and felt himself in Rome, under Diocletian, witnessing the anarchy, conscious of the compulsion, eager for the solution, but unable to conceive whence the next impulse was to come or how it was to act. The two-thousand years failure of Christianity roared upward from Broadway, and no Constantine the Great was in sight."[12]

Both the frontier and the Virgin were racially homogeneous concepts. When Turner insisted to one correspondent that the Wisconsin frontier of his youth served as a melting pot that united disparate peoples, the groups he named —Irish, Pomeranian, Scotch, Welsh, Norwegians, Swiss, and English—were all of Northern European or British descent. He was less enthusiastic about other ethnic clusters entering the country. "There has always been, of course, a considerable immigration of inferior immigrants," he wrote in a 1901 essay for the *Chicago Record-Herald*. "But the more recent immigration of the Jews in startling proportions from congested and miserable regions in Eastern Europe constitutes a new phenomenon." Compounding this problem, he continued, was the Jewish refusal to venture out on the frontier and mesh its culture with that of its adopted country. "The very poverty and consequent congregation of the Russian and Polish Jews into restricted areas of our great cities, and especially of New York, prevents them from assimilating with Americans. Intermarriages with gentiles are so rare that they need to be considered. Religion and language operate powerfully to perpetuate their isolation."[13]

What did the recent influx of new peoples mean to the nation? "It is obvious," Turner soberly reported, "that the replacement of the German and British immigration by southern Italians, Poles, Russian Jews and Slovaks, is a loss to the social organism of the United States." These latter groups avoided the frontier and were by his definition *less* American. In the cities, they remained a people of tightly knit clans, suspicious of the dominant democratic culture, and hostile to free enterprise individualism and social mobility. The cultural divide, Turner argued, explained recent violence between Wasp industrialists and ethnic workers. "During the past fifteen years," he wrote in 1903, "the labor class has been so recruited by a tide of foreign immigration that this new class is now largely made up of persons of foreign parentage, and the lines of cleavage which begin to appear in this country between capital and labor have been accentuated by distinctions of nationality."[14] In sum, the new immigrants frustrated Turner. They rejected what was to him the traditional path of assimilation by refusing to join the centuries-long processional of foraging, frontiering, and farming that melded the dissonant voices of individual groups into one people.

While Turner remained committed to the frontier thesis, Adams's views on historical change took a radical turn in 1900. At that year's Paris Exposition, he observed "the great hall of dynamos"—forty-foot machines that struck him "as a moral force, much as the early Christians felt the Cross." The chaos of the Dynamo, he lamented—speed, change, cities, immigration, confusion—had permanently replaced the unity of the Virgin. As a general hypothesis of historical change, it failed to attract a large audience. Unlike Turner's comforting frontier, Adams's Dynamo was too complex and far too pessimistic for Americans to accept. In 1852, the British physicist William Thomson explained that as energy could only be created by the expenditure of energy, the universe would one day reach a stage of maximum expenditure, reach a stage of entropy and die. Applied to human history, the "speed-up" of time from Neolithic to agrarian, and from mercantilism to capitalism seemed to mirror the inevitable dissipation of the physical world. Too much energy moving too fast. Adams obsessed over the meaning of human existence in a mechanical world where the crush of machines, massing of immigrants and rise of urban towers had overturned the New England of his youth. "Resistance is its law," he wrote of the new power in *The Education*, "and resistance to superior mass is futile and fatal." That book found a select audience in the East, for Adams was not the only displaced patrician searching for meaning in a world alien to his upbringing. It failed to connect, however, with a nation moving into an age of economic and imperial expansion; a nation still basking in youth, still imbued with a missionary impulse, and still confident of its role as a kind of anti-Europe. Turner, who met Adams on a handful of occasions, described the West's rejection of *The Education* as the case of a foreign philosophy failing to connect with the native mind. "Henry Adams was the leader of American historians in his day," he wrote shortly after Adams's death. "His *Education* is a literary classic, an illumination and a tonic—but not normally American."[15]

In its infancy, professional historical writing in America was in need of a popular approach to the past. Amateur historians held the high ground, and their cousins in the academy could broaden their influence only by appealing to a general readership. The tragic, dying fall of the Virgin into the confusion of the Dynamo proved too discouraging for either the professors or the public to embrace. Adams understood this clearly. "If," he declared in his presidential address to the American Historical Association, "the study of history led some scholars to announce that the present evils of the world—its huge armaments, its vast accumulations of capital, its advancing materialism, and declining arts—were to be continued, exaggerated, over another thousand years, no once would listen to us with satisfaction. Society would shut its eyes and ears."[16] But scholars—and society—did rejoice in Turner's frontier hypothesis. It extolled a familiar pioneer archetype, embraced the hallowed American principles of individualism and social mobility, and came along at a time when the Midwest dominated the presidency, the Progressive movement, and made huge strides in industry and the arts. It was a section coming into its own and Turner celebrated its energy. He modified Adams's Virgin—the unifying theme of old Europe—and brought it to the New World. For Turner, the wilderness that he first experienced in his native Wisconsin was a modern, secular force that made not Christians but democrats—the frontier was the American Virgin.

Notes

1. John Franklin Jameson to Frederick Jackson Turner, 7 June 1895, b2, f2, Frederick Jackson Turner Papers, Huntington Library (hereafter cited as FJTPHL).
2. Frederick Jackson Turner to Merle Curti, 8 August 1928, b39, f69, FJTPHL.
3. Elizabeth Donnan and Leo F. Stock, eds., *An Historians World: Selections from the Correspondence of John Franklin Jameson* (Philadelphia, 1956), 46. 1888 was the centennial anniversary of the settlement of the Northwest by citizens of the United States. In recognition of this, the AHA scheduled its annual meeting in Columbus, Ohio in September. The abundance of centennial celebrations in Columbus, however, forced the Association to reschedule its meeting for December in Washington.
4. Ibid., 33.
5. Elizabeth Stevenson, ed., *A Henry Adams Reader* (New York, 1958), 358-9.
6. Frederick Jackson Turner, *The Frontier in American History* (New York, 1920), 205-6.
7. Ray Allen Billington, ed., *"Dear Lady": The Letters of Frederick Jackson Turner and Alice Forbes Perkins Hooper, 1910-1932* (San Marino, 1970), 324.
8. Henry Adams, *The Education of Henry Adams* (1907; revised edition, 1999), 5.
9. Henry Adams, *Mont Saint Michel and Chartres* (1904; revised edition, 1986), 35.
10. Ibid., 7.
11. Ray Allen Billington, "Frederick Jackson Turner Visits new England: 1887," *New England Quarterly* (41), September 1968, 417.
12. Adams, *The Education of Henry Adams*, 499-500.
13. Frederick Jackson Turner to Constance Skinner, 15 March 1922, b4, Frederick Jackson Turner Papers, State Historical Society of Wisconsin; *Chicago Herald-Record*, 16 October 1901.
14. *Chicago Record-Herald*, 25 September 1901; Turner, *Frontier in American History*, 245.
15. Adams, *The Education of Henry Adams*, 380, 493; Wilbur R. Jacobs, *The Historical World of Frederick Jackson Turner: With Selections from His Correspondence* (New Haven, 1968), 54.
16. Stevenson, ed., *A Henry Adams Reader*, 361.

Natural Laws: The Literary and Artistic Roots of American Environmentalism

Patricia Likos Ricci

In 1964, Congress passed the Wilderness Act preserving the last two per cent of wild lands remaining in the United States.[1] Signed by President Lyndon B. Johnson, the law established the National Wilderness Preservation System to acquire and preserve "wilderness areas" according to the following criteria:

> A wilderness, in contrast to those areas where man and his own works dominate the landscape, is hereby recognized as an area where the earth and its community of life are untrammeled by man, where man himself is a visitor who does not remain.... an area of underdeveloped Federal land retaining its primitive character and influence, without permanent improvements or human habitation, which is protected and managed so as to preserve its natural conditions.[2]

The Wilderness Act was a landmark in environmental legislation because it reversed the national policy of permitting private citizens to profit from the land regardless of the consequences to the natural environment. By defining wilderness as "a community of life" endowed with certain unalienable rights, among them, freedom from interference by human beings, the law recognized the moral and legal standing of ecosystems. In doing so, it established scientific, philosophical and legal grounds for the Endangered Species Act passed by Congress three years later. Scientific consensus that habitat loss caused the extinction of species compelled the government to preserve "the ecosystems upon which endangered species and threatened species depend."[3] When President Richard Nixon signed the Endangered Species Act in 1973, he succinctly expressed the intrinsic value of the nation's non-human population. *"Nothing is more priceless and more worthy of preservation,"* Nixon declared, *"than the rich array of animal life with which our country has been blessed."* Nature was still measured by its usefulness to human society, but its life-forms were no longer defined as commodities to be bought, sold and consumed. As the law stated, "fish, wildlife, and plants are of aesthetic, ecological, educational, historical, recreational, and scientific value to the Nation and its people."[4]

Although these newly minted national laws seemed to grow out of the environmental consciousness of the mid-twentieth century symbolized by the founding of Earth Day in 1970, they were in fact an expansion of legal precedents enacted on the state level in the mid-nineteenth century. During decades of intense competition for land and natural resources, the establishment of Arkansas Hot Springs Reservation (1832), Yosemite State Park in California (1864) and the Adirondack Forest Preserve of New York (1885) enshrined a new democratic ideal: that the unique geographic features of the American wilderness were the common patrimony of the present and future citizens of the United States. The New York Legislature asserted the eternal value of wilderness when it proclaimed that "the lands now and hereafter constituting the Forest Preserve shall be forever kept as wild forest lands. They shall not be leased or taken by any person or corporation, public or private." [5] Historian Philip G. Terrie has pointed out that the "forever wild" provision was "a turning point American environmental history, one of those pivotal moments when ideas about the land and the effects of human activity on it reached dramatic fruition." [6] The Adirondacks were, in Paul Schneider's words, "America's first wilderness" in the sense that "here Americans first learned to cherish the wilds as a place of solace and recreation."[7] Why did this environmental ethos emerge in New York? Although there were equally impressive tracts of wilderness in the thirteen original colonies, passionate advocacy for preservation emerged in New York during the first half of the nineteenth century. Linking the cultural capitol of New York City on the eastern seaboard to the seat of government upstate in Albany, the scenic Hudson River Valley became the focus of naturalists, writers and painters.

Decades before Emerson wrote *Nature* and Thoreau composed *Walden*, the writers Washington Irving, James Fennimore Cooper, William Cullen Bryant, and the artist Thomas Cole, founder of the Hudson River School of landscape painters, created an image of wilderness worth preserving.[8] When the Catskills and Adirondacks were still a *terra incognita,* they explored their trackless forests in search of picturesque scenery and sublime vistas. At a time when wilderness was regarded as unfit for human habitation, they demonstrated their kinship with Nature by building homes in the wild, many of which are preserved today as historic landmarks: Washington Irving's *Sunnyside* at Tarrytown, Jasper Cropsey's *Ever Rest* in Hastings-on-Hudson; Thomas Cole's *Cedar Grove* at Catskill, Frederick Church's *Olana* at Hudson, and James Fenimore Cooper's *Otsego Hall* at Cooperstown. Through a campaign waged in publications, exhibitions and lectures, they roused a constituency for preservation based on three principles: first, that wilderness was the distinguishing feature of the America landscape; second, that in so far as all species were made by the Creator, they had a natural right to existence; and third, that civilizations fall when they disregard the natural law of the interdependence of humans and the natural environment.

Land Laws: Divine, Natural and Human

That a wilderness should be set aside for "the benefit and enjoyment of the people" as stated in the law establishing Yosemite National Park (1872) and a place of "health and pleasure" as in the Adirondack State Park (1892) would have seemed preposterous before the nineteenth century. Throughout the history of western civilization wilderness was the place people were least likely to seek out. Once agriculture was invented in the Near East about 10,000 years ago, the idea of wilderness arose to distinguish between cultivated and uncultivated land. Living apart from all the other animals except those they domesticated, humans ceased to be wild; in time, they ceased to think of themselves as animals. So long as they remained within their artificial habitat, humans were securely enthroned at the top of the food chain. Beyond the tilled fields and pasture, however, the wilderness loomed on the horizon, a reminder that their natural predators still lurked in the primordial environment.

Only in the last two centuries have paleontologists reconstructed the prehistory of our species as hunters and gathers adapted to their natural habitat; for more than 1,500 years, the biblical account of human origins as planters and herders was considered authoritative in the West. According to Genesis, the original human habitat was not a wilderness but a garden in the Near East in the vicinity of the Tigris and Euphrates Rivers.[9] The punishing life in the wilds came after Adam trespassed onto the Lord's private property and God cursed the earth and "sent him forth from the Garden of Eden to till the ground from which he was taken."[10] The wrath of God was manifest in the uncontrollable forces of Nature with the power to annihilate all living things with natural disasters and plagues. Tainted by association with the spiritual fall of mankind, the physical hazards of wilderness became analogous to the moral dangers of sin, and therefore something to despise, avoid, or conquer.

Among the creatures, human supremacy was a divine right. Made in the image and likeness of God, Adam was given a moral status that distinguished him from other creatures and the godlike powers of naming the animals and having dominion over them. Every plant, tree, beast, bird, "everything that has the breath of life" was provided as food with the exception of the Tree of the Knowledge of Good and Evil.[11] After Noah preserved the animals from the Deluge, God describes stewardship of the creatures in more oppressive terms: "The fear of you and the dread of you shall be upon every beast of the earth, and upon every bird of the air, upon everything that creeps on the ground and all the fish of the sea; into your hand they are delivered."[12]

Conflicting creation myths regarding human origins contributed to the violent clash of cultures in North America. The Native Americans of the Northeast were primarily a stone-age hunting culture with knowledge of the rudiments of planting. They had no concept of "wild" creatures because they did not domesticate animals, nor did they separate their own origins from the rest of the animals. Attributing souls to all living things, they placed themselves lower in the hierarchy of beings than the totemic animals whom they regarded as ancestors. However, according to the paradigm of biblical man employed by the Puritans, the primeval forest was "a hideous and desolate wilderness, full of wilde beasts and wilde men."[13] Describing Native Americans as *sauvage* (Fr.) or "wilde" (Eng.) gave them the status of animals despite the fact, Washington Irving quipped, that they "walked erect on two feet, had something of the human countenance, uttered certain unintelligible sounds, very much like language; in short, had a marvelous resemblance to human beings."[14] Colonial maps and writings indicate that Europeans recognized the Indians' houses and gardens as villages like their own and acknowledged the role of the Indians in teaching them how to cultivate local crops. William Cronon observed that property law in the Puritan theocracy compelled the Massachusetts Court to recognize the Indians' right to the lands they planted on the legal criteria of "possession or improvement…according to that Gen: 1:28, chap. 9:1, Psa: 115, 16."[15]

In this regard, the most significant difference between the British colonists and the Indians was their mutually exclusive concepts of property. Native Americans did not think they owned the land anymore than the birds owned the sky or the fish owned the sea. Understanding the relationship between a creature and its habitat, they believed that people belonged to a place rather than the place belonged to the people. Unlike the colonial farmers who cultivated crops and raised livestock within legally drawn property lines, the Iroquois and Algonquin peoples were seasonally nomadic hunting tribes dependent on wild animals in habitats with natural boundaries. The villages where they practiced small-scale subsistence agriculture did not obstruct the tracking of game like a fence or a wall, or frighten the animals away like colonial settlements. Because hunting and fishing grounds could be shared without a transferring title, the Indians did not consider the purchase of land to entail exclusive right to occupation. As Cronon explains, "property rights, in other words, shifted with ecological use."[16]

For Europeans, political power and social status derived from hereditary land ownership. Britain's American colonies created unprecedented opportunities to acquire real estate through a variety of alternatives such as purchasing land patents, land grants for military service, homesteading (ownership through "improvement" of the land by erecting buildings or planting crops) or squatting (illegal occupation). Alexis de Tocqueville would later observe that "Americans never use the word *peasant* because they have no idea of the class that term denotes."[17] Furthermore, colonists were free to hunt in the vast forests of America while in England, Isser Woloch noted, "the game laws excluded from the right to hunt not only agricultural laborers, artisans, and tenant farmers, but even wealthy farmers and merchants."[18] Under the monarchies of England and the Continent, forests were royal game preserves and hunting was a privilege of the aristocracy. According to Robert Pogue Harrison, the word *foresta*, from the Latin *forestare*, to keep out, "was originally a [Merovingian] juridical term referring to land placed off limits by royal decree."[19] Deprived of this source of nutrition and income, English peasants openly defied the royal game laws despite the threat of fines and imprisonment which were difficult to enforce.

At the beginning of the seventeenth century, British subjects also faced wood shortages. After fifty years of consuming trees to make charcoal fuel for the iron and glassmaking industries, the depletion of English forests warranted intervention by the Crown. In order to ensure timber for shipbuilding, royal proclamations were issued preserving certain forests from being harvested for firewood, construction, and glass production.[20] These stop-gap measures, like the game laws, generated hostility towards the government without alleviating the problem. The solution was colonization of heavily forested lands populated with "wild and barbarous" people, such as Northern Ireland and New England.[21] Restrictions over natural resources were rapidly replicated in Britain's American colonies where only six years after the Pilgrims landed an ordinance was passed forbidding the export of timber from Plymouth Colony without government permission.[22] In 1691, William and Mary issued a Charter to the Massachusetts Bay Colony reserving the trees twenty-four inches in diameter or greater in the forests of Massachusetts and Maine to furnish masts for the Royal Navy.[23] As in the mother country, British subjects in the American colonies disregarded the ban and two Acts of Parliament did not restrain them from cutting down the towering old-growth pines marked with the broad arrow, the symbol of royal ownership, or violently resisting the enforcement of the timber laws.[24] "The victory of local lumber interests over the wishes of the Crown to preserve the woods for masts," writes John Perlin, "hoisted the flag of independence so many notches higher."[25]

John Locke (1632-1704) addressed the mounting crisis over land use in England in *The Second Treatise on Civil Government* in 1690. Echoing the biblical tradition that "the earth and all that is therein is given to men for the support and comfort of their being," Locke's secular labor theory argued that work, as an extension of our bodies, not only bestowed value onto the land but made it a possession.[26] Therefore the divine injunction to "till the earth" justified the peasants' right to the land they worked, superseding the feudal land-owning practices of the aristocracy. Locke was careful to introduce caveats on the extent of land ownership, advocating that some land be held in common, so that others might pursue their natural rights. Jean-Jacques Rousseau (1712-1778) went farther, denouncing private property as the cause of social injustice in *The Origins of Inequality* (1754). "The first man who, having enclosed a piece of land, thought of saying "this is mine' and found people simple enough to believe him, was the true founder of civil society," Rousseau asserted. "How many crimes, wars, murders: how much misery and horror the human race would have been spared if someone had pulled up the stakes…and cried out… 'You are lost if you forget that the fruits of the earth belong to everyone and that the earth itself belongs to no one!'"[27] Although Rousseau's reasoning would be used to justify the establishment of state and national parks in the following century, the colonial experience of royal monopolies of natural resources left Americans with a lasting antipathy towards the idea of government-owned land that was the greatest roadblock to environmental preservation.

Natural History Revised

In the new republic, few Americans had the foresight to limit deforestation or protect wild animals when a seemingly boundless wilderness stretched from the Atlantic to the Pacific. As long as species were considered immutable and subject to the divinely-ordained stewardship of mankind, their survival did not appear to be in jeopardy.

In 1705, however, the unquestioned belief that mankind had dominion over the Earth since the dawn of creation was called into question when a Dutch colonist stumbled upon a huge tooth on the banks of the Hudson River near the village of Claverack in New York. To explain this bizarre anomaly, the Puritan clergyman Cotton Mather consulted his Bible and, concluding that the enormous molar must have belonged to one of the antediluvian giants mentioned in *Genesis* 6:2, proclaimed the fossils "Lively Proofs of the Mosaic history."[28] In 1739, a hunting party of Native Americans encamped with French-Canadian troops in present-day Kentucky found similar teeth embedded with tusks and a gigantic femur at a site on the Ohio River that came to be known as "Big Bone Lick." According to Adrienne Mayor, the Algonquians knew where to look for the bones of these ancient creatures because fossil ivory was a valuable trading commodity in Native American society.[29] The French commander, Baron de Longueuil, transported the strange specimens to Paris the following year and presented them to the Cabinet du Roi under the direction of the eminent naturalist, Georges-Louis Leclerc de Buffon. Additional fossils of the elephant-like animal exhumed from the Hudson and

Ohio River Valleys in the 1760s found their way into American and British scientific collections where naturalists pondered the similarities in their skeletal structure to the "Mammoths" recovered in Ireland and Siberia. But it was not until 1806, a century after the discovery of the Claverack molar, that the French zoologist Georges Cuvier identified the *American incognitum* as a distinct species which he named "Mastodone," the Greek word for tooth.[30]

Paul Semonin has shown how the mastodon was appropriated as a national symbol during the early years of the republic.[31] For Thomas Jefferson, an avid fossil collector and president of the American Philosophical Society, the colossal creature conclusively disproved Buffon's theory of "American Degeneracy" which asserted that the cold, wet forests of North America could not sustain humans and animals as large or vigorous or diverse as those in Europe. "To whatever animal we ascribe these remains," Jefferson argued in *Notes on the State of Virginia*, "it is certain such a one has existed in America, and that it has been the largest of all terrestrial beings."[32] And to demonstrate the absurdity of the notion "that nature is less active, less energetic on one side of the globe than she is on the other," he called upon American naturalists and fossil hunters to search for a complete skeleton of the *incognitum* in 1799. Two years later, Jefferson's hopes were fulfilled when the Philadelphia artist Charles Willson Peale (1741-1827), curator of the American Philosophical Society's scientific collections, excavated a nearly intact skeleton from Millspaw's Bog in the Hudson River Valley, an event he later commemorated in the painting *Exhuming the Mastodon* (1806-08, Peale Museum, Baltimore). With the guidance of the anatomist Caspar Wistar, Peale rapidly reconstructed the eleven by seventeen foot skeleton and put it on display in the American Philosophical Society. It became the main attraction at Peale's museum in the upper levels of the Pennsylvania State House, later known as Independence Hall.

Founded in 1786, the Philadelphia Museum was a *Wunderkammer* that combined national and natural history, exhibiting portraits of the heroes of the Revolution with specimens of New World animals, minerals, and fossils.[33] In the painting *The Artist in His Museum* (1822, Pennsylvania Academy of the Arts), Peale portrayed himself in the tantalizing act of raising the curtain on the mastodon skeleton while visitors marveled at the exhibition of hundreds of live and stuffed animals. Unlike the European naturalists, he did not display his collection of birds as isolated specimens but arranged them in lifelike poses against painted habitats. One of the earliest ecologists, Peale understood that "by showing the nest, hollow, cave or a particular view of the country from which they came some instances of their habits may be given."[34] Peale's museum of natural history inspired a generation of artists-naturalists to depict American species: Alexander Wilson and Alexander Lawson's *American Ornithology* (1811), Thomas Say's *American Entomology* (1817-28) and *American Conchology* (1830); Richard Harlan's *Fauna Americana* (1825), John Godman's *American Natural History* (1826-28), and James John Audubon's *Birds of America* (1828-38) and *The Viviparous Quadrupeds of North America* (1845-48).

Americans' pride in their natural history was one of the means by which they formed a psychological bond with their homeland. "The biodiversity of each country is part of its national heritage," biologist Edward O. Wilson explains, because "each country possesses its own unique assemblage of plants and animals, including, in almost all cases, species and geographic races found nowhere else." They comprise "the deep history of the national territory, extending back long before the coming of man."[35]

The new awareness of extinction imbued the task of cataloguing American species with urgency unknown to earlier eras. Although Jefferson believed that the *American Incognitum* might still live in the unexplored regions of the west, Lewis and Clark did not come across one during their expedition.[36] Initially the conclusion that fossils were the remains of vanished species was resisted because of its unsettling scientific and theological implications. Buffon had asserted that species were "fixed and constant" until Cuvier convinced him that the only logical explanation for the disappearance of the mastodon was that it had died out.

The mastodon and other fossils called into question the established biblical chronology of the Earth. By adding up the generations of Christ's ancestors in the Old Testament, the Roman Catholic Archbishop James Ussher calculated that the Earth was created about 6000 years before Christ, with Adam's birth occurring in 4004 BC. Using the fossil record, Buffon estimated Earth's age to be at least 75,000 years old in *Des époques de la nature* in 1778. The Scottish geologist James Hutton published supporting evidence in his *Theory of the Earth* seven years later. In 1811, Cuvier and Brogniart devised the stratigraphic method of dating the planet by analyzing the age of the layers of rock in which the mastodon fossils had been found.

"What was this primitive earth?" Cuvier mused. "What was this nature that was not subject to man's dominion?"[37] Despite its "constant laws," Nature was not a system in which "all perishes and all revives," as the *philosophe* Turgot had confidently asserted in 1750.[38] The evidence proved that the Garden of Eden had been replanted with new species many times in the epochs of geological time. Ultimately scientists would have to rewrite the annals of the Earth, adding the long preface of prehistory before mankind was born. In their search for the causes of extinction, they would develop the new fields of paleontology and evolutionary biology. In the final analysis, they would have to decide if humans were subject to the same laws of nature that had extinguished the mastodon.

American History Revisited

The Enlightenment revision of natural history, based on observation rather than revelation, caused a corresponding seismic shift in the understanding of human history. Since the Renaissance, historians had employed the biological metaphor of mortality to explain the succession of civilizations on the world stage against the changing but immortal scenery of Nature. While the progressive "mastery" over Nature by human reason was what distinguished our species from the animals, the human impact on the natural environment was assumed to be slight until the introduction of European civilization into the primeval wilderness of the New World demonstrated the power of technology to transform the natural environment in decades instead of millennia. Although the concept of ecological succession—the replacement of one biotic community by another—was not formulated until the end of the nineteenth-century, the process was clearly observable in the settlement of the United States.[39]

In New York State, where the discovery of the mastodon had generated environmental awareness, the role of humans in transforming ecosystems emerged as a political issue.

Reflecting on the changes wrought by two centuries of colonization, Washington Irving and James Fenimore Cooper applied the new lessons of natural history to American history. Born on the cusp of Romanticism, they were apostles of cultural primitivism who believed with Rousseau that "everything is good in leaving the hands of the creator; everything degenerates in the hands of man."[40] As the first Americans to achieve international reputations, their works quickly attained canonical status but in time the ecological ethos of their original context was forgotten.

Best known for his satires and witty folktales, Washington Irving (1783-1859) was the son of a wealthy British merchant in New York City. Bryant attributed Irving's "strong love of nature" to his childhood rambles around New York City, specifically along the "banks of the Hudson, the extraordinary beauty of which he was the first to describe."[41] Irving's enthusiasm for the Hudson Valley dated at least from 1802-03 when he journeyed up the river to Canada. Having read "that all animals degenerated in America and man among the number," he was anxious to visit Europe where he thought a great man "must be as superior to a great man of America, as a peak of the Alps to a highland of the Hudson."[42] However, his grand tour of England and the Continent in 1804-06 convinced him of the superiority of nature in the United States, for on no country have the charms of nature been more prodigally lavished. Her mighty lakes, like oceans of liquid silver; her mountains, with their bright aerial tints; her valleys, teeming with wild fertility; her tremendous cataracts, thundering in their solitudes; her boundless plains, waving with spontaneous verdure; her broad deep rivers, rolling in solemn silence to the ocean; her trackless forests, where vegetation puts forth all its magnificence; her skies, kindling with the magic of summer clouds and glorious sunshine;—no, never need an American look beyond his own country for the sublime and beautiful of natural scenery.[43]

Irving was admitted to the bar in 1806 and although he did not become an attorney, he utilized his knowledge of the law in his critique of American land policies. The *History of New York from the Beginning of Time to the End of the Dutch Dynasty by Diedrich Knickerbocker* (1809), composed in honor of the 200th anniversary of the discovery of the Hudson River, satirized the cynical manipulation of the enlightened theories of property rights during colonization. Speaking through the fictional Dutch narrator, Irving mocked the transparent self-interest behind the legend that New York, "when first visited by Europeans, was a howling wilderness, inhabited by nothing but wild beasts; and that the transatlantic visitors acquired an incontrovertible property therein, by the *right of discovery*."[44] If property rights were "acquired by *cultivation*," Knickerbocker argued, then the Indians had no claim to America:

> In entering upon a newly-discovered, uncultivated country, therefore, the newcomers were but taking possession of what, according to the aforesaid doctrine, was their own property—therefore, in opposing them, the savages were invading their just rights, infringing the immutable laws of Nature, and counteracting the will of Heaven—therefore, they were guilty of impiety, burglary, and trespass on the case—therefore, they were hardened sinners against God and man—therefore, they ought to be exterminated. [45]

Irving's mockery of the founding of New Amsterdam included a stinging indictment of the colonists' destruction of the original ecosystem. "Think you the first discoverers of this fair quarter of the globe had nothing to do but go on shore and find a country ready laid out and cultivated like a garden, wherein they might revel at their ease? No such thing," Knickerbocker writes, "they had forests to cut down, under-wood to grub up, marshes to drain, and savages to exterminate."[46] In contrast, when Henry Hudson and his crew first laid eyes on Manhattan Island "no signs of human thrift appeared to check the delicious wildness of Nature, who here reveled in all her luxuriant variety." The hills "were then adorned with the vigorous natives of the soil—the lordly oak, the generous chestnut, the graceful elm—while here and there the tulip-tree reared its majestic head, the giant of the forest."[47] He imagined "those happier days of our city, when as yet New Amsterdam was a mere pastoral town, shrouded in groves of sycamores and willows, and surrounded by trackless forests and wide-spreading waters, that seemed to shut out all the cares and vanities of a wicked world."[48]

While Irving acknowledged that nostalgia idealized the past like a landscape melting into the distance, James Fenimore Cooper's darker view of American history (1789-1851) was based on his childhood experiences on the frontier. His father, William Cooper, was a land speculator who made a fortune in central New York in the land rush that followed General John Sullivan's defeat of the Iroquois in 1779. He established the frontier settlement Cooperstown on Otsego Lake and, as landed gentry in the power vacuum of the wilderness, soon became the chief judge of Otsego County and a Congressman. Raised in Cooperstown, James Fenimore Cooper witnessed the power struggles over natural resources and the competition for land among the different classes of humans and the varieties of animals. In 1820, after brief and unsuccessful stint at Yale and in the Navy, he began writing the historical novels that won him lasting international fame. Cooper's passionate advocacy for the preservation of wilderness evolved in the *Leather-Stocking Tales—The Pioneers* (1823), *The Last of the Mohicans* (1826), *The Prairie* (1827), *The Pathfinder* (1840) and *The Deerslayer* (1841)—a series of novels that follows the development of wilderness from the first settlements in the Northeast to the westward expansion taking place during his lifetime. The importance of laws protecting the natural environment was the subject of his autobiographical novel, *The Pioneers* in 1823.[49] In the frontier village of Templeton at the end of the eighteenth-century, Nathaniel Bumppo, an old displaced frontiersman known as "Leather-Stocking" for his Indian garb, informs the town's founder, Judge Temple, that the settlers have already "driven God's creatures from the wilderness." Game is becoming scarce because of their "wasty ways" of living on the land: their axes destroy habitats by turning "good hunting-grounds into stumpy pastures"; their seines catch hundreds of fish, most of which are left to rot on the shore; their rifles and swivel cannon cruelly massacre pigeons in flight, "firing into flocks of God's creatures in a wasty manner, to kill twenty and eat one." With no appreciation of the gifts of Nature, they mindlessly chop down ancient sugar maples for firewood instead of preserving them for syrup or their beautiful wood. In contrast, Leather-Stocking, like the Indians whose lifestyle he follows, only kills what he eats. Ironically, when Judge Temple introduces game laws to conserve wildlife, Bumppo is arrested for shooting a single deer out of season.

Nelson Van Valen contends that the "first major struggle between utilitarian and preservationist was not that between [Gifford] Pinchot and [John] Muir over California's

Yosemite National Park but the almost equally famous, albeit fictional, contest between two equally redoubtable antagonists, Marmaduke Temple and Nathaniel Bumppo, over New York's Lake Otsego Wilderness."[50] Van Valen sees this philosophical conflict as a representation of "the striking ambivalence in Cooper's conservation commitment," but in the Preface to the 1832 edition of *The Pioneers* the author explicitly expresses his concern with the preservation of wildlife. "Though forests still crown the mountains of Otsego, the bear, the wolf and the panther are nearly strangers to them," Cooper wrote. "Even the innocent deer is rarely seen bounding beneath their arches, for the rifle and the activity of the settlers have driven them to other haunts."[51] Since the animals belonged to the same ecosystem as the Native Americans, Cooper anticipated that they would suffer a similar fate when the forest was destroyed. Fittingly, Indian John, the last of the Mohicans, makes his appearance in *The Pioneers*. Paul K. Johnston noted that "Cooper's *The Pioneers* is a crucial text in American cultural history in that it served to transform the Puritans' Biblical notion of wilderness into the secularized yet nevertheless still sacred notion of wilderness that became increasingly important in American culture in the nineteenth and twentieth centuries."[52] In *The Deerslayer*, the conclusion to the *Leather-Stocking Tales*, the religious conviction at the core of Cooper's environmentalism surfaces in his description of Natty as one "who sees God in the forest; hears him in the woods; bows to Him in the firmament;…a being who finds the impress of the Deity in all the works of nature, without any of the blots produced by the expedients, and passion and mistakes of man."[53]

Kindred Spirits

William Cullen Bryant (1794-1878) shared Cooper's reverence for wilderness and his belief in its moral perfection. "The primal curse fell, it is true, upon the unsinning earth," he wrote, "but not in vengeance."[54] The son of a learned physician and state representative, Bryant was born in Cummington, Massachusetts where he practiced law after studying at Williams College. An attorney by profession but a poet by disposition, Bryant's precocious talent was recognized when the *North American Review* published "Thanatopsis" with its exhortation to follow "Nature's teachings" in 1821. Hailed as the "American Wordsworth," Bryant discovered his "Lake Country" in the Hudson Valley in 1825 when he abandoned his law practice to become editor of the *New York Review*. "How much I admired the shores of the Hudson above Canal Street," he recalled, "where the dark rocks jutted far out into the water, with little bays between, above which drooped forest-trees overrun with wild vines."[55] In New York Bryant met Cooper, who had recently published *The Pioneers,* and he joined Cooper's "Bread and Cheese Club," a weekly meeting of writers and artists. Surrounded by talented, like-minded associates, Bryant published *The Talisman* in 1828, the first of a series of handsome gift-books extolling the glories of the American wilderness.[56] In the following years, the engravings in *American Scenery, Picturesque America*, and *The Home Book of the Picturesque* gave readers a virtual tour of the Catskills and Adirondack Mountains, the Palisades of the Hudson River, Lake George and Niagara Falls, places they would later be called upon to defend.

One of Bryant's earliest poems was *Inscription for an Entrance to a Wood* and it presaged a lifetime commitment to forest preservation. As a writer and editor, Bryant may have been influenced by John Evelyn's *Sylvae, or Discourse on Forest Trees* (1664), a scientific treatise on reforestation originally published by the Royal Society of London to address the timber shortage in England that had gone into several editions, including an illustrated version in 1825. To encourage his countrymen to conserve their forests, Evelyn wrote a history of trees throughout civilization and described their spiritual, philosophical, and social contributions to humanity. He emphasized the high regard in which they were held by the ancient cultures that preserved them in sacred groves. For centuries, the British had harvested their forests without replanting and by 1783, the increase in the industrial demand for timber and charcoal had reduced England's abundant forests to a mere 51,500 trees.[57]

Bryant's concern that America not be shorn of her primeval forest is expressed in the poem "Earth," where he exclaims "My native Land of Groves! a newer page in the great record of the world is thine; shall it be fairer?" In "A Forest Hymn," he introduced Americans to the idea that the sacred groves of antiquity were "God's first temples."[58] In the poem "Among the Trees," he reminds the reader that they are also alive by addressing them, "Trees of the forest, and the open field! Have ye no sense of being?" One of the original "tree-huggers," he used personification to generate empathy for the giants of the forest as they were being cut down. "Do there not run strange shudderings through your fibres when the axe is raised against you, and the shining blade deals blow on blow, until with all their boughs, your summits waver and ye fall to earth?"[59] The British philosopher Jeremy Bentham had employed this strategy to make the case against cruelty to animals in 1789: "The question is not, Can they reason? Can they talk?" Bentham argued, "but Can they suffer?"[60]

From 1829 until his death in 1878, Bryant used his position as editor of the *Evening Post* as a bully pulpit to preserve the wilderness in New York. He successfully lobbied for the passage of the State Park Act of 1851 and the establishment of national forest preserves in 1865. "It has been suggested, by persons who can think of something else besides railroads," he wrote in the *Evening Post*, "that it will be an act of provident wisdom to reserve considerable tracts of forest in different parts of the country, as the public domain, with a view of preventing the destruction of trees which is so rapidly proceeding..." The objections that forest protection was unenforceable because "what is in the public domain is regarded in most parts of our country as, in a certain sense, common property," he recommended "a body of foresters to watch it and keep out trespassers...retained in the pay of the Government."[61]

Bryant's close relationship with the painter Thomas Cole (1801-1848) was memorialized in *Kindred Spirits* (1849, New York Public Library), a double-portrait of the poet and the late painter conversing on a promontory above a river gorge in the Catskill Mountains painted by their mutual friend, Asher B. Durand. "Of Cole, I vividly remember the interest with which his works were at that time regarded," Bryant recollected. "Here, we said, is a young man who does not paint nature at second hand.... Here is the physiognomy of our woods and fields; here are the tinges of our own atmosphere; here is American nature and the feeling it awakens."[62] Neither affluent, nor well-educated, nor even American, Cole was a different species than the writers and painters he met in New York. He was born in the industrial town of Bolton, Lancashire where his father struggled to manufacture textiles until 1818 when the family immigrated to Steubenville,

Ohio. In his new home, Cole, who had apprenticed as a calico designer in England, aspired to become a portraitist and in 1823 he traveled to Philadelphia to study at the Pennsylvania Academy of the Fine Arts founded by Charles Willson Peale. In contact with the peculiar blend of art and science that characterized Peale's institutions, he found the subject on which he built his career: the American landscape. In 1825, Cole made the first of what would become an annual summer trip to sketch in the Catskill Mountains. Armed with these drawings, he returned to New York City and produced a few paintings of wilderness that determined the course of American painting for the next fifty years. Daniel Huntington, president of the National Academy of Design, recalled that Cole "studied to embody whatever was characteristic of the singular grandeur and wildness of mountain, lake and forest in the American wilderness."[63] In subtle ways, these early landscapes evoked the new American literature. The barely visible Indian brave standing on the rocky ledge of *Falls of the Kaaterskill* (1826, Warner Collection) alludes to Washington Irving's retelling of the creation myth of the waterfall and the startled deer that glances at the viewer out of the *Lake with Dead Tree, Catskill* (1825, Allen Memorial Art Museum) evokes the opening hunting scene of James Fenimore Cooper's *The Pioneers*. Cole's desire to emulate the successful American historical novelists became explicit in 1827 when he painted a landscape with a *Scene from the Last of the Mohicans* (Fenimore Cooper Museum). He must have learned quickly from Cooper that the wilderness he was discovering was endangered because he suddenly began painting the thinly veiled religious allegories, *Landscape Composition: St. John in the Wilderness* (1827, Wadsworth Athenaeum) and *The Expulsion from the Garden of Eden* (1827-28, Boston Museum of Fine Arts). "It seems certain that Cole intended to draw an analogy between Biblical history and the providential history of the United States," Tim Barringer writes, noting that Cole himself is quoted as saying "We are still in Eden, the wall that shuts us out of the garden is ignorance and folly."[64]

At the time, Americans were in the process of chopping their way out of Eden. By the 1830s, about 1,600 acres of wilderness were being removed per year.[65] The dramatic transformation of the American landscape prompted Alexis de Tocqueville to reflect on the implications of the imminent destruction of the wilderness when he visited the United States in 1831:

> We are perhaps the last travelers who will have been allowed to see it in its primitive splendour, so great is the force that drives the white race to the complete conquest of the New World.... It is this consciousness of destruction, this arrière-pensèe of quick and inevitable change that gives, we feel, so peculiar a character and such a touching beauty to the solitudes of America. One sees them with a melancholy pleasure; one is in some sort of hurry to admire them. Thoughts of the savage, natural grandeur that is going to come to an end become mingled with splendid anticipations of the triumphant march of civilization. One feels proud to be a man, and yet at the same time one experiences I cannot say what bitter regret at the power God had granted us over nature.[66]

For President Andrew Jackson, the clearing of the wilderness was a cause for celebration. "What good man," he asked in his Inaugural Address, "would prefer a country with forests ranged over by a few thousand savages to our extensive republic, studded with cities, towns and prosperous farms, embellished with all the improvements art can devise or industry execute?"[67] A cultural elite in Paris, London and New York might wish to preserve the wilderness for its intangible spiritual and aesthetic qualities, but to the typical American homesteader, it was a dangerous obstruction; to the industrialists, it was a valuable commodity.

Thomas Cole became an advocate of wilderness preservation during the Jackson Administration (1829-1837). In 1835, he published an *Essay on American Scenery* in which he refuted Jackson's argument for the elimination of wilderness on nationalistic, aesthetic and religious grounds. Citing the prophets and hermits of the Bible, Cole reminded his readers that wilderness was God's creation. "The good, the enlightened of all ages and nations have found pleasure and consolation in the beauty of the rural earth,"[68] while those who are "consumed in the low pursuits of avarice...are unconscious of the harmony of creation."[69] They destroyed the landscape "with a wantonness and barbarism scarcely credible in a civilized nation."[70] Moreover, the idea that man could improve on God's creation was preposterous to Cole. On the contrary, he maintained that the landscape was "desecrated by what is called improvement which generally destroys Nature's beauty without substituting that of Art."[71]

The contrast between the Old and New World landscapes was particularly striking to Cole who had grown up in England when it was the least forested country in Europe.[72] In the Ohio Valley where Cole's family settled in 1818, naturalists had measured colossal oaks, walnuts and sycamores with six to seven foot diameters.[73] By 1836, *The View from Mount Holyoke, Northampton, The Oxbow of the Connecticut River* (Metropolitan Museum of Art) showed a valley entirely cleared for farming with scattered trees and scraps of forest remaining on the hilltops. Cole's most persuasive argument may have been his assertion that "the most distinctive...and impressive characteristic of American scenery is its wildness because in civilized Europe the primitive features of scenery have long since been destroyed or modified—the extensive forests that once overshadowed a great part of it have been felled...and to this cultivated state our western world is fast approaching."[74]

Paradise Lost : *The Course of Empire*

Cole's hopes and fears for the future of his adopted country under the policies of the Jackson Administration were expressed in *The Course of Empire* (1836; The New York Historical Society), a series of five paintings depicting "the History of a Natural Scene, as well as an Epitome of Man; showing the *natural* changes of Landscape and those effected by Man in his progress from Barbarism to Civilization—to the state of Luxury—to the vicious state of Destruction etc."[75] The ecological interpretation of *The Course of Empire* distinguished it from previous essays on the rise and fall of civilizations. By portraying a single location over the span of human history, Cole illustrated the irreversible process of historical and environmental succession that results in the extinction of a civilization. In accordance with enlightened scientific opinion, his chronology began with the recently discovered prehistoric stage. In the beginning was the wilderness, peopled with Neolithic hunters who resemble North American Indian tribes. In this "Savage State" at the dawn of civilization, the human species is immersed in the fecundity of wilderness. The invention of agriculture produces the "Pastoral State" in which land is cleared for farming and people live in small rural communities. Agriculture increases population growth, generating complex urban environments represented by "Consummation," an imperial capital at its zenith. Imperialism initially produces wealth and luxury, but instigates wars of conquest that create tyranny at home and enmity abroad. "Destruction" shows the inevitable annihilation of the empire through wars of reprisal. The final stage is "Desolation" in which the ruins of civilization are gradually reclaimed by Nature. Considered by James Fenimore Cooper to be "one of the noblest works of art that has ever been wrought," *The Course of Empire* raised the disturbing issue of whether the downward trajectory of past civilizations was preventable.

In 1864, the pioneer ecologist, George Perkins Marsh, published empirical evidence that supported Cole's environmental theory of history.[76] A friend of William Cullen Bryant and an art collector, Marsh was familiar with *The Course of Empire* and adopted Cole's terminology in his book, *Man and Nature, or Physical Geography Modified by Human Action* (1864). In the original "Savage State," Marsh explained, the whole earth had been a forest where "the simpler people recognized a certain community of nature between man, brute animals, and even plants." The impact of these hunters and gatherers on the natural environment was slight in comparison with the farmers who actually changed the surface of the earth.[77] In the "Pastoral State," the practice of clearing land for raising crops and grazing domesticated animals sustained a greater human population but extensive deforestation resulted in infertile, arid soil that led to food shortages and imperialistic wars to replenish natural resources.[78] According to Marsh, the empires that combined the "ignorant disregard of the laws of nature" with "brutal and exhausting despotism," ultimately destroyed both the state and the environment.[79] By this means, the ancient civilizations had "brought the face of the earth to a Desolation almost as complete as that of the moon."[80] "Nature's laws" Marsh concluded, "are as inflexible in dealing with an atom as with a continent or a planet."[81] Wilderness preservationists deployed *The Course of Empire* theme in the following decades. "We are following the course of nations that have gone before us," warned a forestry expert in *Harper's Magazine* in 1882, " Europe and Asia have been as reckless in their destruction of the forests as we have been and...have brought upon the land itself barrenness and desolation."[82]

Paradise Regained: The Preservation Movement

After Cole's death in 1848, the Hudson River School shifted its environmental strategy from the conservation to the preservation of New York's forests. In the 1830s, before the region was even surveyed, Cole and Durand had traveled into the Adirondacks to sketch and the opportunity to paint sublime scenery like Cole's *Schroon Mountain* attracted artists to the Adirondacks for the rest of the century. By 1850, New York had become the largest producer of lumber in the nation.[83] The sanctity of property rights in the United States made it clear that the only way to preserve wilderness was to own it. In 1856, the editor of The *Crayon*, William Stillman, organized The Adirondack Club, a group of painters and writers who purchased 22,500 acres in the Adirondacks for the use of the members.[84] The following year, Samuel Hammond, an Albany lawyer and journalist, called for legislation. "Mark out a circle a hundred miles in diameter and throw around it the protective aegis of the constitution," he demanded. "It should be a misdemeanor to chop down a tree, a felony to clear an acre...the old woods should stand here always as God made them."[85] In 1870, New York State created the Adirondack Forest Preserve, stipulating that it should be kept forever as wild forest lands."[86] Advocates of wilderness preservation employed Cole's strategy of representing the same scene before and after human interference in *The Course of Empire*. "A Feeder of the Hudson—As it was" and "A Feeder of the Hudson—As it is" engraved by Julian Rix for *Harper's Weekly* in 1885 graphically portrayed the deleterious effects of deforestation on streams and rivers.[87] In 1892, the Adirondack State Park was established "to protect forest land necessary to the preservation of the headwaters of the chief rivers of the State."[88] And in 1894, the voters finally approved a constitutional amendment prohibiting the sale of forest land and the removal of timber.[89]

The sublime landscapes of the Adirondacks continued to inspire preservationists into the 20th century. Robert Marshall, who founded The Wilderness Society in 1935, grew up in the Adirondacks. "Wilderness," he wrote, "furnishes perhaps the best opportunity for pure aesthetic rapture."[90] Howard Zahniser, who had defended the Adirondack Preserve in the 1940s, drafted the first federal wilderness bill. "We deeply need the humility to know ourselves as the dependent members of a great community of life," he wrote.[91] After nine years of hearings, Congress passed the Wilderness Act in 1964, securing the "enduring resource of wilderness" for future generations of Americans.[92] The riches of wilderness were redefined as the health benefits of outdoor recreation, the spiritual rewards of communion with wild creatures, the scientific value of studying the ecology of a primordial environment, and the preservation of nation's natural beauty. The principles of natural law that had liberated the Indians and the slaves, and women and children, from the category of property were finally applied to wild animals and wild lands, granting them the right to life and liberty which, in the words of the Declaration of Independence, "the Laws of Nature and of Nature's God entitle them."

Notes

1. This essay is a development of a paper "Natural Laws: The Hudson River School and the Preservation of Wilderness" presented at the College Art Association Annual Conference, 2000.
   The authoritative study is Roderick Nash's *Wilderness and the American Mind*, (New Haven: Yale University Press, 1967) now in its fourth edition (2001). For the history of the Wilderness Act of 1964 see Chapter 12: "Decisions for Permanence," 200-212.
2. Philip G. Terrie, *Forever Wild: Environmental Aesthetics and the Adirondack Forest Preserve*, (Philadelphia: Temple Univesity Press, 1985)10.
3. Endangered Species Act, 1973, states in Sec. 2 A: "Congress finds and declares that-(1) various species of fish, wildlife, and plants in the United States have been rendered extinct as a consequence of economic growth and development untempered by adequate concern and conservation; (2) other species of fish, wildlife, and plants have been so depleted in numbers that they are in danger of or threatened with extinction; and (4) the United States has pledged itself as a sovereign state in the international community to conserve to the extent practicable the various species of fish or wildlife and plants facing extinction; and (5)b. The purposes of this Act are to provide a means whereby the ecosystems upon which endangered species and threatened species depend may be conserved, to provide a program for the conservation of such endangered species and threatened species, and to take such steps as may be appropriate to achieve the purposes of the treaties and conventions set forth in subsection (a) of this section.
4. Endangered Species Act (1973), Sec.2 A: "Congress finds and declares that-(3) these species of fish, wildlife, and plants are of aesthetic, ecological, educational, historical, recreational, and scientific value to the Nation and its people"
5. Terrie, 97.

6. Terrie, 3.
7. Paul Schneider, *the Adirondacks: A History of America's First Wilderness,* (New York: Henry Holt & Co., 1997) xi.
8. Emerson's essay *On Nature* dates from 1836; Thoreau's *A Week on the Concord And Merrimac River* from 1849. *Walden* was published in 1854.
9. In the Genesis 2:10-14, two of the four rivers flowing out of Eden are identified as the Tigris, east of Assyria, and the Euphrates. Quotation from Gen. 1:28.
10. Gen 3:23.
11. Gen.1:29-31.
12. Gen.9:1.
13. Nathaniel Morton, New England's Memorial (Boston, 1826), 35; quoted by Alexis de Tocqueville in *Democracy in America*, 1835, (New York: Alfred A. Knopf, Inc., 1994) Vol. 1; 34.
14. Washington Irving, "A History of New York from the Beginning of the World to the End of the Dutch Dynasty by Diedrich Knickerbocker," *The Works of Washington Irving,* (New York: A.L. Burton Co., 1900) Vol. I; 46.
15. William Cronon, *Changes in the Land: Indians, Colonists and the Ecology of New England,*(New York: Hill & Wang, 1991) 63.
16. Cronon, 63.
17. Tocqueville, *Democracy in America,* 316.
18. Isser Woloch, *Eighteenth Century Europe: Tradition and Progress, 1715-1789* (New York: W.W. Norton & Co., 1982) 175f.
19. Robert Pogue Harrison, *Forest: The Shadow of Civilization,* (Chicago: University of Chicago Press, 1992) 69.
20. John Perlin, *A Forest Journey,* (Cambridge, Massachusetts: Harvard University Press, 1989) 193.
21. Wood exporter Sir Henry Wallop's description of the Irish to Queen Elizabeth I, quoted by Perlin, 197.
22. "A Plymouth Colony Ordinance Forbidding Export of Timber, March 29, 1626," Frank E. Smith, ed., *Conservation in the United States: A Documentary History,* Vol. 1, "Land and Water, 1492-1900," (New York: Chelsea House, 1971) 3.
23. Perlin, 287.
24. See Perlin's history of this dispute, "New England: Seeds of Independence," 286- 301.
25. Ibid. 301.
26. In Chapter 5, "Property," Locke cites Psalm CXV.16; John Locke, *The Second Treatise on Civil-Government* 1690; ed. Thomas P. Peardon, (New York: Macmillan, 1952), 16.
27. Jean-Jacques Rousseau, *A Discourse on Inequality,* 1754; trans. Maurice Cranston, (London: Penguin Books, 1984) Part 2, 109.
28. Paul Semonin,, *American Monster: How the nation's first prehistoric creature became a symbol of national identity.* (New York & London: New York University Press, 2000) 30.
29. Adrienne Mayor, *Fossil Legends of the First Americans,* (Princeton: Princeton University Press, 2005).
30. Semonin, *American Monster,* 355.
31. See Semonin's introduction, "Patriotism and Prehistoric Nature," 1-14.
32. Buffon's theory of "American Degeneracy," published in *Histoire Naturelle, générale et particulière,* (Paris: Imprimeries royale, 1749-1788) is debated by Jefferson in *Notes on the State of Virginia* 1781-82, ed. Merrill D. Peterson, *Writings: Thomas Jefferson 1743-1826* (New York: Library of America, 1984) 169-172.
33. The definitive study is Charles Coleman Sellers, *Mr. Peale's Museum: Charles Willson Peale and the First Popular Museum of Natural Science and Art* (New York: Norton, 1980). Peale's museum survives today as the Academy of Natural Sciences in Philadelphia.
34. Ibid, 28.
35. Edward O. Wilson,"Biophilia and the Environmental Ethic," *In Search of Nature,* (Washington, D.C.: Island Press, 1996) 176-8.
36. In *Notes on the State of Virginia,* Jefferson expresses skepticism about extinction: "Such is the oeconomy of nature, that no instance can be produced of her having permitted any one race of her animals to become extinct…"; Peterson, 176.
37. Georges Cuvier, "Memoir on the Species of Elephants, Both Living and Fossil," 1796; quoted by Semonin, 302.

38. Anne-Robert-Jacques Turgot, "On the Successive Advances of the Human Mind,"1750; in *The Portable Enlightenment Reader,* ed. Isaac Kramnick, (New York: Penguin Group, 1995) 361.
39. University of Chicago Professor Henry Chandler Cowles is credited with introducing scientific evidence for ecological succession in his pioneering study "The Ecological Relations of the Vegetation of the Sand Dunes of Lake Michigan" in the *Botanical Gazette* in 1899.
40. Jean-Jacques Rousseau, *Emile, or On Education* 1762, trans. Allan Bloom, (New York: Basic Books, 1979) Vol. 1, 37.
41. William Cullen Bryant, "Washington Irving," *Prose Writings*, ed. Parke Godwin, (New York: Russell & Russell, 1964) vol. 1, 336.
42. Washington Irving, "The Author's Account of Himself," *The Works of Washington Irving,* Vol. I, 8.
43. Ibid.
44. Irving, *A History of New York,* 46.
45. Ibid. 47.
46. Ibid. 38.
47. Ibid. 76-77.
48. Ibid. 88.
49. Quotes are taken from James Fenimore Cooper, *The Pioneers,* introduction by Donald A. Ringe, (New York: Penguin Books, 1988).
50. Nelson Van Valen, "James Fenimore Cooper and the conservation Schism," *New York History,* Vol. LXII, No. 3 (July 1981) 290.
51. Cooper, *The Pioneers,* 9.
52. Paul K. Johnston, "A Puritan in the Wilderness: Natty Bumppo's Language and America's Nature Today," *James Fenimore Cooper: His Country and His Art,* ed. Hugh C. MacDougall, (New York: New York University Press, 1997) 60.
53. John J. McAleer, "Biblical analogy in the Leatherstocking Tales," *Leatherstocking and the Critics,* ed. Warren S. Walker, (Chicago: Scott, Formena & Co., 1965) 127.
54. William Cullen Bryant, "Inscription at the Entrance to a Wood," *Poetical Works of William Cullen Bryant* , (New York: D. Appleton & Co., 1908), 24-25.
55. Bryant, *Prose Writings*, 336.
56. For gift-books of American scenery, see Georgia P. Barnhill, *Wild Impressions,* (Boston: The Adirondack Museum with David R.Godine, 1995) 41-61.
57. Perlin, 245.
58. Bryant, "A Forest Hymn,"1860, *Poetical Works*, 79-82.
59. Ibid., "Among the Trees" 1868, 321-25.
60. Roderick Frazier Nash, *The Rights of Nature: A History of Environmental Ethics,* (Madison,, Wisconsin: University of Wisconsin Press, 1989) 23.
61. Bryant, *Prose Writings*, 1964, vol. 2, "The Utility of Trees"(*Evening Post,* June 20, 1865), 402.
62. Ibid. "The Academy of Design" (April 28, 1865), 232.
63. Louis Legrand Noble, *The Life and Work of Thomas Cole,* 1853; ed. Elliot S. Vessell, (Cambridge: Harvard U. Press, 1964) 57.
64. Andrew Wilton and Tim Barringer, *American Sublime: Landscape Painting in the United States 1820-1880,* (London: Tate Publishing, 2002) 93.
65. Perlin, 356.
66. Alexis de Tocqueville, *Journey to America 1831,* 399; quoted by Barbara Novak, *The Natural-Paradise: Painting in America, 1800-1950* (New York: Museum of Modern Art, 1976) 62-63.
67. President Andrew Jackson, "Second Annual Message," quoted in Nash, *Wilderness and the American Mind,* 41, n. 57.
68. Cole's "Essay on American Scenery" is reprinted in *American Art 1700-1960: Sources and Documents* ed. John McCoubrey, (Englewood Cliff, N.J.: Prentice-Hall, Inc., 1965) 99.
69. Ibid.
70. Ibid 109
71. Ibid.
72. Stephen Daniels, "The Political Iconography of Woodland in Later Georgian England," *The Iconography of Landscape*, ed. Denis Cosgrove, (Cambridge: Cambridge University Press: 1989) 43.
73. Perlin, 325-326.
74. Cole, "Essay on American Scenery," 102.

75. See Angela Miller, "Thomas Cole and Jacksonian America: The Course of Empire as Political Allegory", *Prospects,* Vol. 14, 1989, 65-92; Ellwood C. Parry III, *Thomas Cole's The Course of Empire: A Study in Serial Imagery* (Ann Arbor: Yale University Dissertations, 1991); Allan Wallach, "Thomas Cole's Landscape and the Course of American Empire" in *Thomas Cole: Landscape into History*, (New Haven and Washington DC: National Museum of American Art, 1994).
76. For Marsh, see David Lowenthal's Introduction to George P. Marsh, *Man and Nature, or Physical Geography as Modified by Human Action (1864)*, (Cambridge: Harvard University Press, 1965)
77. Ibid. 114; n.36; 37.
78. Ibid. 40.
79. Ibid. 11.
80. Ibid. 42.
81. Ibid. 464.
82. N.Egleston, quoted in Perlin, 361.
83. Frank Graham, Jr., *The Adirondack Park*, (NY: Alfred Knopf, 1978), 15.
84. Barbara Novak, *Nature and Culture: American Landscape and Painting 1825-75* (New York: Oxford University Press, 1980) 65.
85. Graham, 16-17.
86. Terrie, 92f.
87. Terrie, 118; fig.13; 119, fig.119.
88. For the history of this legislation, see Graham, 119-126.
89. For Article VII, No.7, amendment to the New York State Constitution, see Terrie, 92-109.
90. Nash, 2001; 203.
91. Ibid. 214.
92. Ibid. 224.

What Worlds are Made Of:
The Lakota Sense of Place

David Martínez

    How did the world come to be the way it is today? And out of the infinite number of places in which a people could have lived, how did they wind up where they are now? How do they know where they belong, if they have a home at all, and what accounts for their strong attachment to a given place? For the Lakota, the answers are found in the story of the Four Winds. What follows then is neither a work of ethnography, nor will it address the ongoing legal issues surrounding Lakota land claims. Instead, what I am attempting to do is analyze Lakota land relations for the precepts and values that this tradition expresses, particularly in its creation mythology. For it will be through storytelling, especially of the creation story, that a uniquely Lakota sense of place will be expounded.

    By a sense of place I mean, of course, more than a capacity for spatial orientation but a realization of homeland. More specifically, I am referring to what occurs when one perceives a particular place as being one's home. As A. Irving Hallowell argues, "There is no 'spatial sense,' equivalent to vision and hearing, by means of which we perceive" the attributes of space. "Such experience is 'intersensory' by its very nature; yet is as primary as experience mediated by specialized sensory modalities."[1] Knowing one's homeland, then, is a matter of being aware of oneself in relation to traditional reference points in the surrounding landscape. What this suggests is that a homeland is not only defined by concrete landmarks, but also by the mental map that one retains of this place. The mental map, in turn, is made up of kinetic memories, which themselves may be organized around symbolic sites. The symbolism inherent in the landscape suggests that awareness of one's homeland is not limited to physical boundaries, but rather expands into cosmic domains, including the sky, the stars, perhaps an underworld, and a mythic past. In the story of the Four Winds, the Lakota invoke a transcendent realm, Wakan Tanka, which consists of the four most sacred beings: Wi, the Sun, Skan, "that which moves everything," Maka, the Earth, and Inyan, the Stone. Each one of these wakan beings would acquire a companion, because everything desires companionship as an antidote to loneliness. Together they would establish the world as it is known by the Lakota today, which they would represent in a variety of everyday and ceremonial structures, from the tipi to the Sun Dance site.

As Maije Kūle observes in her phenomenological analysis of home, "Home is not the physical space in which we live." On the contrary, home is one of the spiritual spheres in which one dwells, which is contiguous with family, culture, and language. As such, a sense of home entails the fulfillment of a fundamental need to have somewhere to always return, and in which one can find stability, harmony, and an opportunity to express oneself.[2] Because home is such a basic need of the human condition, when one has a home, it is prone to being taken for granted. Frequently, it is only when a home is lost or taken away that one realizes the intensity of the attachment to such a place. In the meantime, with respect to stability and harmony, Edward S. Casey points out in *Getting Back Into Place*, "*at home* we do not usually have to confront such questions as 'Where am I?' 'Where is my next meal coming from?' or 'Do I have any friends in the world?'"[3] Having a home therefore means being completely attuned to one's surroundings, knowing how to gain sustenance, and being recognized and accepted by the others around one. What we learn from the Lakota, in particular, is that the right to a given place entails more than claiming a legal title to it; rather, it involves making a valid claim of destiny. In other words, a people had to be here because they could not have become who they are now anywhere else. This is why stories like the one about the four sons of Tate are told with a certain anticipation for the arrival of humans, but not just any humans. Instead, they are the people who speak the language in which their story is told.

Before there were humans, there was only Inyan, Maka, Skan, and Wi. The memory of such a time is preserved in myth, which is really the story of archetypal beings, who express the values and beliefs of a people. Although there are variations on this story, including the length of the story, the characters involved, and the events that transpired; nonetheless, all versions are anchored by some common presumptions. More to the point, the Lakota entered a world determined by the sons of Tate, the Wind, who would establish the four directions. In *The Sons of the Wind*, edited by D. M. Dooling, we read that these four brothers, Yata, Eya, Yanpa, and Okaga were instructed by their father to set out for the edge of the world.[4] By virtue of their ordeals, each wind not only found a direction, they each found a home. They would do so with Wazi's help, a wizard who was condemned to wander the edge of the earth for having taken part in a conspiracy against the wakan beings to make them look foolish. Skan told Wazi that he could enter the world if he assisted Tate's sons on their mission.

Wazi told the four brothers that he could help them travel farther and faster by giving them moccasins, which they had never worn before. In the far distance there was a hill, which Wazi offered to take them to in leaps and bounds. Yata was suspicious of Wazi and was reluctant to accept the offer. Eya, however, took Wazi up on his proposition and soon found himself at the foot of the hill. When the other three brothers finally arrived, they all heard terribly thunderous noises coming from atop. All were afraid except for Okaga, who volunteered to go ahead and investigate. He found a curious round lodge that had an opening on top but no doors. Next to this were a great cedar tree and a huge nest containing an enormous egg. Okaga heard someone drumming in the lodge, while he could hear something pecking in the egg. As Okaga approached the lodge a frightening voice asked him who he was and what he wanted around here. Okaga answered with his name and an explanation of his brothers' mission. The voice told Okaga that he and his brothers may pass. Okaga then beckoned his brothers, telling them it was safe.

When Eya came along he was transfixed by what he saw. The voice asked him what he wanted. Eya said that he wanted to know more about the great being who was in the lodge. A sparrow then flew out. Eya was astonished to see such a small creature after hearing such a terribly thunderous voice. The sparrow then said to Eya, "This is the lodge of Wakinyan, the winged one, and that great voice is his voice. I am his messenger and forerunner. Whoever looks at him becomes a *heyoka* and forever must speak and act in an opposite manner. Do you still wish to look at him?" said the swallow."[5] Eya accepted, but the sparrow told him that if the Wakinyan became displeased with him, he would strike and be killed. On the other hand, if the Wakinyan was pleased with Eya, he would become his companion. On both counts, Eya accepted the opportunity to see the Wakinyan. A shapeless being like a cloud of smoke then emerged. "His body has no form," as Lame Deer would describe him, "but he has huge, four-jointed wings. He has no feet, but he has claws, enormous claws. He has no head, but he has a huge beak with rows of sharp teeth."[6] Eya looked on and became a heyoka, acting in a contrary way, including shouting very disrespectful things to the great Wakinyan. The Wakinyan responded by being pleased with Eya, telling him that he did not have to be a heyoka any longer. The Wakinyan then gave his blessing to Eya and his brothers. They could proceed with their mission. But upon its completion, the Wakinyan said, Eya would no longer live with his father. Instead, the Wakinyan said to Eya: "Your tipi shall be upon my mountain, beside my lodge. Together you and I will purify the world from all filthy things. We will sweep and wash it, and water the ground. We will cause all things that grow from the ground to flourish and bear leaves, flowers, and fruits…. This has been my task from the beginning. Now you will help me, and all that breathes will be grateful to us."[7] Eya was then told to return to his brothers because Yata's birthright had been given to him. Because Yata had been rude and cowardly around Wazi, Eya would get to mark the first direction as his own. It would only be after the whites arrived that this place would acquire the name of Mount Harney in the Black Hills.[8] But before this transition would take place, each of the four brothers would found a direction, with Yata taking the north, Yanpa the east, and Okaga the south. Each would mark their direction with a pile of stones and, in turn, each direction would be affiliated with a particular bird, a color, a guardian animal, and even a season. With respect to what the four brothers would accomplish, the sparrow told Eya:

> The directions you will fix will be the only things in the world that are immovable. When going toward any of these directions, mountains, valleys, rivers, forests, or plains will sometimes be on one side, and sometimes on the other, but the direction will forever remain in one place.[9]

The four directions, however, will not become abstract points, such as those pinpointed by a compass. Instead, we could say about the Lakota directions what A. Irving Hallowell said about the Saulteaux perception of place, that the directions were contingent upon the peculiarities of key natural phenomena. The Saulteaux believed like the Lakota that the four winds were brothers, who each had a home in their respective directions. Moreover, because they were anthropomorphic deities they not only established the cardinal directions that the Saulteaux would need to orient themselves to their homeland in Manitoba, but also established a personal relationship with the people. According to Saulteaux mythology, the east wind was the first-born, who declared that he would be fairly kind to humans, while the south wind said that he would always be very good to humans and treat them well. The west wind asserted in turn that he would be a bit rough on humans but never wicked. Lastly, the north wind proclaimed that he would always be rough on humans.[10] We find a similar arrangement in the Lakota story of the four winds. When the four brothers were born they each manifested the characteristics that would define them for all time. "As they named Yata," the story goes, "he scowled at them. As they named Eya he yawned and waved his arms. As they named Yanpa he slept. And as they named Okaga he smiled and laughed."[11] Looked at this way, the homes of the four winds are place-names in a very real sense, as opposed to being fully abstract points on a map.

Yi-Fu Tuan, in his book *Space and Place*, interprets the above practices as examples of spatial imagination that is endemic to myth. More specifically, Tuan argues that all humans express an intuitive grasp of the world beyond their direct experience. Imagination does not end at the boundaries of one's homeland, but rather is catalyzed into imagining the unknown. At least, the realm of the unknown is such when compared to direct, everyday experience. The realm of the unknown is in fact known through the stories told about persons who have traveled beyond the boundaries of the everyday. Such stories are recounted in both myth and in personal dreams and visions. The impact that this has on one's concept of homeland is that both people and land are perceived as sitting at the center of the universe. In the case of the Lakota, Wi, Skan, Maka, Inyan, and their companions, ultimately exist to make the world inhabitable for humans. The Lakota may owe Wakan Tanka gratitude for such a possible world; but the fact that such a world exists with humans in it means that there is a meaningful place here for them. What Tuan says about oriented mythical spaces in general is thereby true for the Lakota. "It organizes the forces of nature and society by associating them with significant locations or places within the spatial system," such as the Black Hills to the west or Pipestone to the east. "It attempts to make sense of the universe by classifying its components and suggesting that mutual influences exist among them," such as the changing seasons accounted for by the ongoing battle between the cantankerous north wind, Yata, and his three brothers. "It imputes personality to space, thus transforming space in effect into place," such as the prairie being thought of as Wohpe's dress. Lastly, oriented mythical space "is almost infinitely divisible—that is to say, not only the known world but its smallest part, such as a single shelter, is an image of the cosmos."[12] Even before the Lakota emerged onto the surface of the earth, the wakan beings, including the four winds and the Wakinyan, lived in lodges and tipis. With respect to the tipis once used by the Lakota, William K. Powers points out in *Oglala Religion* that the floor plan of an Oglala tipi is oriented with respect to the mythical four winds. Powers writes:

> ...we see that the *catku*, or place of honor, is located at the west; the women's side is at the north, or on the left (from the perspective of the *catku*); the *tiyopa*, or doorway, is at the east; the men's side is at the south, or right (again viewed from the *catku*)...[13]

According to Powers, this corresponds to the instructions that the four brothers received about where each one should go to found their respective directions, as well as the tension that ensued after Yata lost his birthright, giving rise to the four seasons. More specifically, the four brothers were told to go places according to their relationship with the sun, or *Wi*. "The North Wind," Powers notes, was told to go "where his shadow is longest at midday, the West Wind to where the sun goes over the mountain when the day is over, the East Wind to where the sun comes up at the edge of the world to begin his journey, and the South Wind to where he is under the sun at midday."[14] With respect to the tipi, the south wind, or Okaga, is identified with the hearth in the middle. Powers interprets this as a holdover from the times when the Lakota were more sedentary. In other words, the relation between the four winds mythology and the tipi expresses symbolically a recognition about the necessities of food production, and thereby of life itself. This is to say that there is a vital confluence of forces represented by the sun, which is associated with the east wind, the warmth of the south wind, and the rains of the west wind, which are brought in by the Wakinyan, the great thunder-being. Powers continues his analysis by pointing out:

> Similarly, it is logical to place the seat of honor at the west in recognition of the first-honored direction, the doorway at the east where the first light is emitted, and the fireplace in the center for maximum heat. The sun is literally over the fireplace (roughly) at midday.... The fireplace itself is a shallow pit...the idea of placing the South Wind, which symbolized creativity, not only of food but of humankind, in this particular spatial relationship agrees with other rituals and myths in which creativity or revivification is related to concavities in the earth.[15]

In the creation story, the Lakota came up from below the surface of the earth through a cave. They were enticed by the many wonderful things they could enjoy here, not the least of which was the taste of buffalo meat. "Tatanka," who was also a wise man for the people below the earth's surface, "warned the people that those who passed through the cave could never again find the entrance, and must remain on the world. He said that winds blew on the world and were cold; that game must be hunted, and skins tanned and sewed to make clothes and tipis."[16]

When the people came up through the cave, they forgot the language of the spirits that they once spoke and how to serve them. Tatanka followed the people to the surface so that he could help them. But upon entering the world, Tatanka turned into a shaggy buffalo. Tatanka, however, remembered the language of the spirits, while the people invented a new tongue for themselves that other creatures could not understand. They were now the *Ikce Oyate*, the Real People. "They were the first people on the world, and the Lakota are their descendants."[17] According to legend, the Lakota were once a single community who made their winter camp at Sacred Lake, which was suspected by James Walker of being the Mille Lacs region of Minnesota. This was the original center of the world. Eventually the people would grow and divide into various bands, who would live within the world founded first by the four brothers. Modern history, of course, would change the Lakota landscape even more drastically.

Nevertheless, as Tuan affirms in his analysis of homeland attachments, "Cosmic views can be adjusted to suit new circumstances." Despite the incursion of westward expansion and the concomitant displacement of the Ikce Oyate by the Ojibwe in the

Mille Lacs area, the Lakota perception of being centered within a mythologically defined world endured. For the center that really mattered was not tied exclusively to a particular physical site. This does not mean that having to abandon a place is easy; on the contrary, it can be quite demoralizing. Still, recuperation depends on maintaining the cohesion of the group, as well as the mythical value of the center, which can be re-established wherever the people reside. Moreover, the people must feel that their deities or guardian-spirits are still with them. An important sign that attachment has taken place is that the land is as a nurse and mother to the people. If this relationship emerges, then the people will recognize themselves as a part of the land. They will see their culture and history in the landmarks around them. As Tuan observes:

> Landscape is personal and tribal history made visible. The native's identity—his place in the total scheme of things—is not in doubt, because the myths that support it are as real as the rocks and waterholes he can see and touch. He finds recorded in his land the ancient story of the lives and deeds of the immortal beings from whom he himself is descended, and whom he reveres. The whole countryside is his family tree.[18]

The Lakota homeland is such a place. It is where they emerged as a people. It is where they learned many things for the first time from Tatanka, Wazi, and Wakanka. The Black Hills, in particular, is where they were reborn as a people after Unktehi flooded the world and killed all of the people except for a lone girl. She was rescued by an eagle who gave her a son and daughter, who would later generate a new people, an eagle nation.

In the end, what the Lakota concept of homeland demonstrates is that attachment to a given place does not simply depend on being the dominant force in that area. Although the Lakota were once very powerful, the legitimacy of their claim to a given homeland was based on the amount of care they put into this place. Care is different from labor, which is the Lockean criterion for ownership. For care is an expression of love, a concern for another, as opposed to a desire for exploitation, which only facilitates personal gain. The Lakota care for the land as for a person by recognizing spirits all around them. In turn, they practice a religion that honors these spirits, and seeks from them, through such ceremonies as the Sun Dance, the revivification of themselves and their home. What Casey says about the relation between caring and place in *Getting Back Into Place* can be said about the Lakota. Casey states, "We care about places as well as people, so much so that we can say that *caring belongs to places*. We care about places in many ways, but in building on them—*building with them*, indeed, *building them*—they become the ongoing "stars of our life," that to which we turn when we travel and to which we return when we come back home."[19]

Notes

1. A. Irving Hallowell. "Cultural Factors in Spatial Orientation," in *Culture & Experience*. (Philadelphia: University of Pennsylvania Press, 1955), p. 185.
2. Maije K le. "Home: A Phenomenological Approach," in *Passion for Place Book II: Between the Vital Spacing and the Creative Horizons of Fulfilment*. Anna-Teresa Tymieniecka (ed.). (Dordrecht: Kluwer Academic Publishers, 1997), p. 97ff.
3. Edward S. Casey. *Getting Back Into Place: Toward a Renewed Understanding of the Place-World*. (Bloomington: University of Indiana Press, 1993), p. 121.
4. D. M. Dooling (ed.). *The Sons of the Wind*. (New York: Parabola Books, 1984), p. 30.

5. *The Sons of the Wind*, p. 64.
6. Richard Erdoes and John Fire. *Lame Deer: Seeker of Visions*. (New York: Simon and Schuster, 1971), p. ???
7. *The Sons of the Wind*, p. 65.
8. William K. Powers. *Sacred Language*. (Norman: University of Oklahoma Press, 1986), p. 37.
9. *The Sons of the Wind*, p. 66.
10. *Culture & Experience*, pp. 190-191.
11. *The Sons of the Wind*, p. 30.
12. Yi-Fu Tuan. *Space and Place: The Perspective of Experience*. (Minneapolis: University of Minnesota Press, 1977), p. 91.
13. William K. Powers. *Oglala Religion*. (Lincoln: University of Nebraska Press, 1982), p. 177.
14. *Oglala Religion*, p. 176.
15. *Oglala Religion*, p. 177.
16. *The Sons of the Four Winds*, p. 121.
17. *The Sons of the Four Winds*, p. 122.
18. *Space and Place*, pp. 157-158.
19. *Getting Back Into Place*, pp. 175-176.

An Feochàn

Matt Willen

*"Oh, there is blessing in this gentle breeze
That flows from the green fields and from the clouds
And from the sky."—The Prelude, 1805 text,* William Wordsworth

In the landscape of traditional Irish music, there is a classification of composition that is referred to as the slow air. Although some experts in the field of Irish traditional music might insist that properly the term refers to the melody of a slow song or ballad, it is frequently used to refer to any slow melody, often (though not always) performed unaccompanied, whether or not it was originally composed for a song. "An Feochàn" is the title of such a slow air, which is perhaps not surprising since in English its title means "a gentle breeze." A song-less air composed by the inimitable Sligo fiddle player Tommy Peoples, "An Feochàn" is a haunting melody whose first part gently blows along a current of tones that stir from the bottom of the first octave and swell in frequency and degree to its upper reaches and settle slowly back to the calm of its origins at the base of the octave in much the same way that a breeze draws itself across your body, buffeting your hair, your skin, your clothes, gently at first, and then it rises with intermittent bursts that get stronger and more frequent but never quite become a full wind, before it subsides to a still, quiet rest. The second part of the air begins with a sudden gust from the top of the first octave that crests briefly at the apex of the second octave where it wavers unsteadily, dropping briefly a half-tone before rising again to its crest, from which it subsides, slowly, through the first octave, again to a still, quiet rest.

I came across "An Feochàn" as the result of an afternoon spent rummaging through the international music section of the public library's compact disc collection in an effort to broaden my own collection and experience of traditional Irish music. There among the stacks of recordings by Carlos Montoya, Tibetan monks, klezmer bands, and Brazilian choro musicians, I found a compilation of music performed by the Irish band Altan, The First Ten Years: 1985-1994. *The next day, while driving along the Pennsylvania turnpike, I slipped the disc into the cd player and listened as the commanding renditions of traditional and original tunes and songs for which the band is known surged from the speakers, until the disc switched to track 8, when such a slow and haunting air played on solo flute by the late Frankie Kennedy began to blow that I had to pull over and stop on the verge of the road to listen. To continue driving suddenly seemed inimical to the experience of listening to the air, from which I could sense something otherworldly. There I felt something stir though it was difficult to tell if what stirred was in the car or inside of me, and I imagined being carried off to a place far away. I listened once, and then again, before returning to the world of the road I was traveling and the rush of air as it blew by the car windows.*

To hear a slow air played well is a spiritual experience in a sense that is not inconsistent with the reference to the breeze that Wordsworth invokes in the opening lines of *The Prelude* (the epigraph to this essay) and throughout the rest of his autobiographical poem. There *is* blessing in the movement of a slow air that breathes life into the soul, that inspires and renews, and that opens windows onto forms of experience (musical or otherwise) that we would otherwise find inaccessible. Although "An Feochàn" (a gentle breeze) is a slow air, one might say conversely that slow air is a gentle breeze. In a well-known essay from the eighties on the presence of "air-in-motion, whether it occurs as breeze or breath, wind or respiration" in Romantic poetry (25), the literary critic M. H. Abrams explains that in *The Prelude* the breeze appears as "the stimulus and outer correspondent to a springlike revival of the spirit after a wintry season, and also to a revival of poetic inspiration which Wordsworth [...] equates with the inspiration of the prophets when touched by the Holy Spirit" ("Correspondent Breeze" 28). He cites the following passage as illustration:

> For I, methought, while the sweet breath of heaven
> Was blowing on my body, felt within
> A corresponding mild creative breeze,
> A vital breeze which traveled gently on
> O'er things which it had made, and is become
> A tempest, a redundant energy,
> Vexing its own creation. 'Tis a power
> That does not come unrecognized, a storm
> Which, breaking up a long-continued frost,
> Brings with it vernal promises...
> The holy life of music and of verse...
>
>   To the open fields I told
> A prophecy; poetic numbers came
> Spontaneously, and clothed in priestly robe
> My spirit, thus singled out, as it might seem,
> For holy services.
>   (Cited in "Correspondent Breeze" 29; from 1805 text, I, 41-63)

The association between breathing and breezes is certainly explicit here, if not somewhat confounded since it is a breath which blows against the poet's body (a heavenly breath) and a breeze that blows within. Abrams goes on to discuss in his essay that the association of breezes and breath and spirit, soul, or inspiration is not something that originated with the Romantic poets (although their use of it was in response to the specific cultural conditions of their time); the relationship between these different forms and effects of moving air can be traced both etymologically and historically back to the Greeks. Less apparent though is the suggestion in *The Prelude* that within the poet there exists a landscape which the inspirational breeze "traveled gently on/ O'er things which it had made." The nature of this inner landscape is difficult to ascertain or to map with any sort of precision. But from this landscape originates music and verse, which the spirit in its "holy service" gathers and invests with life. That is to say that not only is the encounter with the external breeze a spiritual experience but the act of artistic creation that it gives rise to is equally as spiritual, and biblically speaking perhaps even more so since it involves investing inanimate things with life, the creation of the "holy life of music and verse."

Not long after I first heard it, I got hold of a transcription of "An Feochàn" and learned to play it on the pennywhistle. I wanted to go to that place that Frankie Kennedy had carried me to, to create it myself, and settle there for as long as I liked. I practiced it for weeks, making sure that I could play it without hitting any bad notes, that I could ornament the melody at a couple of places that called for it, that I could get the timing down just as it was transcribed before I played it out, which I did one Friday evening at a Borders bookstore where my friend was promoting a disc he had just recorded. I played it that night on a B flat whistle, the only instrument I had that could sound anything even remotely close to the flute that Kennedy used to play it. I played it twice through, nailing it on both occasions, hit all of the notes cleanly with exception of one, that octave long leap in the second part on the first time through (a mistake soon forgotten). But when I finished I knew that it was desperate, that it had none of that lightness that air has to it, that the flame of candle would not have flickered had one been in the room. I simply got through it, in much the way I used to compose sonnets in the creative writing classes I took as an undergraduate student, when the most important things to getting it right were iambic pentameter, fourteen lines, and rhyme schemes. What more can you do than simply get through it when you believe that's all there is to it?

Although the slow air employs many of the same rules and conventions of musical composition as the reels and jigs and hornpipes and other classifications of tunes that comprise the extensive geography of traditional Irish music, its performance capitalizes on what is referred to in the lexicon of classical music as a *rubato* style of playing (which entails lengthening and shortening the duration of notes freely and expressively) and on a range of ornamentation, dynamics, and other sorts of embellishment to achieve various harmonic and melodic effects to a degree that those other tune classifications do not. More so than following a melody that can be whistled or hummed, it follows a course that begins at the musician's heart and gathers its momentum and fluctuations from the spirit of the occasion for its performance. Consequently, the transcription of a slow air is, *at best*, a rough sketch, a gesture towards the shape of a melody that is about as accurate as a meteorological chart of pressure systems and air currents; it delineates general tendencies but cannot map the particularities and nuances of individual living bodies of air because these are always changing, taking their shape and form from the landscapes over which they travel.

At the Sheebeen in Westport Quay one night, I watched a man pump the bellows of his Uilleann pipes and blow life into an unfamiliar air, and it was unlike anything I had heard before. I could feel the melody as it blew over my body, as it stirred inside, and I became aware of something being sounded inside me that reached a depth that I had never known before. As the melody progressed, the pub settled into stillness and silence. Some people closed their eyes. Some leaned forward and rested their elbows on their knees, allowing their heads to hang loosely as leaves hang from a tree. The melody coursed through the room the way an evening breeze lilts over fields of flowers and tall grasses. A candle on the mantle flickered. The shadows it cast swayed. The embers in the fireplace glowed red, and the flames bent and trembled like blown blades of grass.

There is a passage in Ciaran Carson's *Last Night's Fun: In and Out of Time with Irish Music* in which a nameless pundit speaking of judging fiddling competitions comments on the playing of slow airs: "There's many's a one who can play the reels and the jigs, but it's the slow air that'll sort them out" (93). There is a difficulty to playing the slow air that is different from playing a dance tune, and this is perhaps because the objective of playing the slow air is not simply to play a melody but to achieve what Rilke has referred to as a "holy departure," a placing of the inner most point of the musician's self outside as a place no longer habitable:

> You stranger: music. You heart-space
> grown out of us. The deepest space in us,
> which, rising above us, forces its way out,—
> holy departure:
> when the innermost point in us stands
> outside, as the most practiced distance, as the other
> side of the air:
> pure,
> boundless,
> no longer habitable.

That's to say that the objective is not simple self-expression, or even, as Rilke suggests elsewhere in this poem, the expression of feelings, although expression is certainly an important part of the objective. Simple self-expression is a euphemism for narcissism. "God does not give us graces or talents or virtues for ourselves alone," Thomas Merton reminds us. (56) Brian Hartigan has written in the liner notes to *With Friends Like These* that James Keane, a virtuoso accordion player from Drimnagh, County Dublin, "draws much of his inspiration from the belief that traditional music is more than a mere pastime or entertainment, but rather, in a very real sense, it is the living history of the Irish people—a chronicle embedded in sound, of everything that has gone on up to this moment and, as such, must be treasured by each succeeding generation" (1). In the sense that Hartigan speaks of Keane's inspiration, the objective of playing this music is also about breathing life into a history. But it is a different sort of history than what we read in books, for its stories are told in a language that is not language, and it paints a landscape that cannot be seen. It is a history of the Irish spirit as it blows through and lives within the individual musician, and which he or she conveys and imparts upon playing.

I've heard it said—though I'm not sure where for the words come to me as if out of a dream of a pub one night in Teelin, or Doolin, or Dublin, from the space between sets of tunes, a place filled with the raising and lowering of glasses and the murmur of voices blending and telling so long you'd think the music wasn't it at all—that to play the slow air you need to place yourself at the interstice between breeze and wind and balance there as on a rope suspended between birches that bend and sway back and forth, back and forth.

As with any other form of spirituality there are two fundamental practices that make this "holy service," as Wordsworth called it, possible; that allow the musician to create what Rilke has called a "holy departure," the placing the of the innermost point inside of us "outside, as the most practiced distance." These are devotion and faith. On the one hand, the musician needs to devote himself to his art which is essential to make playing the air possible. It entails developing technical expertise on an instrument, and acquiring knowledge of the musical tradition; it is a matter of discipline, though I hesitate to use the word 'discipline' because of its (often justified) negative connotations. I have in mind, instead, the sense of discipline as something that makes things possible, much as the disciplined breathing practices in Yoga, for example, make possible a certain form of transcendence. Devotion in this sense is more like what Hartigan has called, again with reference to the spiritual nature of James Keane's playing, "a joyous devotion —tremendously uplifting, self-renewing, and triumphantly alive" (1).

Last evening, I walked outside to watch the sun go down beyond the fields behind my house. There was a breeze that brushed lightly against my skin. So delicate was it that when I looked about I could see no sign of it! Not a blade of grass quivered. Not a single leaf swayed. The few clouds, rippled and red on the horizon, remained still and unchanged through the duration of the sun's descent. Still I could feel a breeze, invisible in every way, as it brushed by and cooled me.

Faith on the other hand has to do with belief, what Thomas Merton has said we "assent to [...] because of something other than intrinsic evidence" of its results (127). The musician needs to believe in the existence of something that is not empirically verifiable, something that cannot be seen or charted, or even to some extent recorded because the character of a slow air arises as well from the environment in which it is performed, just as the breeze that blows over meadows carries the invisible fragrance of flowers with it—something, that is, is captured in the recording but something, its living moment, is lost as well. There is an other-world to Irish traditional music, not visible or readily accessible, in which the musician needs to believe; an Ireland whose landscape is shaped by the melodies that an individual knows, whose places, inhabitants and their experiences are commemorated by those melodies. A musician needs to be able to enter that landscape and summon its spirit, to know the quality of the breeze that blows across it, a breeze that blows in from the west sodden with Atlantic moisture, that drags itself across peat bogs and caresses the cracks and niches of stone cottage remnants half-dissolved from years of rain and wind, remains of castles and abbeys whose walls lay in heaps where the land meets the sea, where the hills and the grasslands touch the sky, a breeze steeped in fuchsia and foxglove; and to know how the quality of that breeze differs, for instance, from the summer breeze that rises at night in the desert southwest which cracks and snaps over sand and stone as it bristles through the branches of creosote, mesquite, pinon, and juniper, through red rock canyons and along cliff faces, the habitat and home of people who vanished a thousand and more years ago. To invoke Merton again, faith "incorporates the unknown into our own life in a living, dynamic and actual manner" by integrating "the unknown and the known in a living whole" (136).

At ten o'clock I walked in the door and out of myself, and took up a seat on a wooden bench that spanned the back walls of the Cul a Duin, where I spent the night amidst a flurry of jigs and reels and hornpipes—and there was an air, "The Dawning of the Day" —and pints of Guinness, and hours talking with a woman named Kitty who had spent her eighty plus years in Teelin, and who knew everyone and whom everyone knew, and who could tell you in just the right terms to make you feel how the west wind is fierce in late autumn when it blows winter in from the Atlantic, and how many people had been blown from One Man's Pass on Slieve League, and who sang a beautiful song when called upon, and who clenched her fists and showed her appreciation by thrusting them into the mighty wind let lose by eight fiddlers and a young woman on button accordion and an ex-patriot on the bouzouki and an American on the mandolin, and who called out, "Yes, play it well," and who said, "Ah, you have the music," when I offered a set of "Home Ruler" and "Kitty's Wedding" that I picked up from a disc by Noel Hill and Tony Linnane a couple of years back because I liked what I heard and wanted to go there as well.

At the dawning of the day I left the pub and walked the mountain road that climbs above Donegal Bay along the rocky flanks of Slieve League rising up against a cobalt sky. The bay was a sea of clouds. I wandered through crag and mist, and wondered about fairies and about how many musicians must have strayed or stumbled up this road in the early morning after a session to stand on the edge of the mountain, let their hair blow in the breeze, and look out to the mountains south of the bay and to the Atlantic in the west. Then I hitched a ride from Kitty and her niece to the inn where my travel companion Bill, who had retired earlier in the morning, slept firm. Later that morning on our way to the next night, we drove to the old town site of Port on the Atlantic coast. We walked the trail above the sea cliffs and watched as the slightest breeze tore the remaining morning mists into shrouds on the razor edges of sea-soaked crags, and lifted the scent of low tide and the music of the surf as it beat on the shore like it has done for millennia. The town of Port was no town at all, only the remnants of an old fishing village and a slip for launching boats. Then and there it seemed quite logical that the Gaelic word port *translates to* tune *in English, for we had many hours ago entered into a world of music, and here, at the place where the land meets the sea, and the air moves in you as much as around you, and all that remains of a town site are ruins and memories and a breeze that veils them with mist, is where you learn to play the slow air.*

References

Abrams, M.H.. "The Correspondent Breeze: A Romantic Metaphor." *The Correspondent Breeze: Essays on English Romanticism* (New York: W.W. Norton and Company, 1984), 25-43.

Carson, Ciaran. *Last Night's Fun: In and Out of Time with Irish Music* (New York: North Point Press, 1996).

Hartigan, Brian. "Liner Notes." *With Friends Like These*. James Keane et al. Shanachie Records 78015, 1997. 1-4.

Merton, Thomas. *New Seeds of Contemplation* (New York: New Directions Books, 1972).

Rilke, Rainer Maria. "To Music." *Ahead of All Parting: The Selected Poetry and Prose of Rainer Maria Rilke*. Ed. and Trans. Stephen Mitchell (New York: Modern Library, 1995), 143.

Wordsworth, William. *The Prelude,* 1805 version. In *The Prelude: 1799, 1805, 1850*. Ed. Jonathan Wordsworth, M.H. Abrams, and Stephen Gill (New York: W.W. Norton and Company, 1979).

On the Line of the Horizon: Anxiety in de Chirico's Metaphysical Spaces

Andreas Philippopoulos-Mihalopoulos

The Line the Eye Sees

The horizon fascinates the eye, while imposing an ordeal on the mind. The line of the horizon augurs the beginning of eventuality, where the possibility is materialised as ineffability; but at the same time, it sends the eye "before," back on itself, in the whiteness of its sleep, in destinations past and desires swallowed, creeping up Nietzschean bodies of *Übermenschen* and relentlessly battering their brain with the possibility of the end. It is on the very line of the horizon, line and non-line at the same time, where impossibility becomes materialised as the possibility of the end. Thus, beginning and finality palpitate on the solitude of the line separating the visible from the *au-delà*.

The term "visible" is not, of course, coincidental. The division between "here" and "beyond" on the basis of visuality may be arbitrary (why this amongst others?), but potentially justified. Visuality is the expression avenue of the politics of presence par excellence, the other senses assuming a fundamental but antithetical role in the process of self-situating. They assist, as it were, in the fixing of positioning, but they are differently directed. By this, I would not want to suggest that they are to be less trusted. On the contrary, mechanisms of greater confidence in the subtlety of the non-visual(!) are constantly being negotiated. However, one would be tempted to observe that the "inadequacy" of, say, the olfactory or the aural, is conferred precisely on the basis of their more-than-compensatory role in what could lead to more "enigmatic" quests than that of presence. It is on their reverse basis, therefore, as a negation of presence, or as enablers of Heideggerian moods, that these senses should be sought and employed. Here, however, the quest is defined at first instance almost entirely by a mediated visuality. Giorgio de Chirico's paintings will be brought in the discussion as essays on the meaning of landscape, as well as examples of the horizon's functional multiplicity, which will then be interdigitated with the words of Søren Kierkegaard in an attempt to situate the "enigma" of De Chirico in relation to Kierkegaardian anxiety. One should not, however, rush to condemn the fact that the reconstructing of the atmosphere of such paintings will be based solely on words, at best evoking mnemonic constructs if one is familiar with de Chirico paintings or at least the thematology of an Italian piazza, and at worst constructing readings and echoes of readings in the mind of the reader. The reason is the following: words are capable, no doubt to a limited extent, to evoke the "other" side too, whichever that may be, whose description is more readily facilitated by sensory stimulations other than the visual. I wish I could include a "scratch-here" patch somewhere in the text—I would, however, be at a loss as to what odor the patch should reveal. It is solely through words then. And hopefully the reader will have no trouble constructing the visual, along with the other sensory perceptions, based on her ability to imagine what lies before and beyond the line of the horizon. Because here, the visual, together with the other senses, will be mustered in their mediated textual apparition, as ways of projected reality (what Husserl would call *phantasy*), in order to echo within the reader a certain *Stimmung*, an atmosphere of reception, construction, belonging and losing oneself in one's environment. For this is perhaps, if not the only, at least a certain tried way in which emotions can be understood but not rationalised. This is partly the reason for which the following text should be taken neither as art criticism, philosophical treaty, verbose pastime or existential scream—exclusively. Thus, the partial performativity of the present piece can hopefully be forgiven, rather than rejected as another word game.

Landscape

De Chirico created dream landscapes. After having read Nietzsche's *The Birth of Tragedy*, and in a conscious attempt to represent the Apollonian incantation of another, altogether different reality lying underneath, de Chirico expands his canvas to accommodate the metaphysics of everyday. Nietzsche wrote of the "Apollonian state of dreams in which the world of the day becomes veiled, and a new world, clearer, more understandable, more moving than the everyday world and yet more shadowy, presents itself to our eyes in continual rebirths."[1] De Chirico's landscapes are fractions of recurrent dreams, imposed one atop the other in a frenzied heterotopia, creating syntheses of perspectives, surfaces, light sources, shadows and differentiated temporal zones, all overflowing the canvas in performative fireworks, and assailing the viewer with anxieties of every sort, with the ultimate aim to produce the question (the "enigma," as the demiurge likes to call it) that is posited once the phenomenal world is revealed simply as a theatre stage,[2] as another narrative which leads into the question while leading away from the answer. The canvases are *disorientating*: faithful to his Nietzschean influences, de Chirico confounds the viewer's visuality and *sense* by offering *non-sense*, a multiplicity of eyes clustered together for the joyful abandonment to a certain fate: since "reality is intolerable"[3] it is the task of the artist to reverse it and replace it with a tolerable world. And this, de Chirico does it slyly: "De Chirico's great achievement was effortlessly to combine incompatible spatial systems into one seemingly coherent image, which only on closer inspection is revealed to be fraught with inconsistencies and internal contradictions."[4] Indeed, at first instance, one sees an admittedly empty and rather desolate piazza, a rather frequent occurrence in Italian cities. Still, such a landscape manages to disorient and disquiet, and this can greatly be attributed to the palimpsestic nature of de Chirico's spatiotemporal treatment of the landscape, with his falsified perspectives and disjointed planes. The viewer is lost in a piazza that prima facie looks "normal," coherent, real. It is only then, once the feeling of anxiety has been apprehended, that the viewer begins enquiring into the nature of the cause of anxiety, and realises that nothing seems to match, yet everything seems well positioned: the arches flanking the piazza end up in different vanishing points; the statue in the middle of the piazza looks as if seen from below; the figures in the background float about in an immaterial vastness, unconnected with the rest of the piazza; the edges of the city stop abruptly and give way to deserted expanses that seem to reflect a vertiginously collapsing sky. "The objective forms of reality seem to be juxtaposed, each with its own vanishing point and none exhibiting any logical or organic relationship with the next. Each element creates and occupies its own space and, without being strictly representational, acquires meaning to the extent that it gives rise to a feeling of pure presence."[5] All is there, present, supposedly meaningful unto itself, naturally positioned; but nothing makes sense.

This *non-sense* is partly what de Chirico was referring to when talking about his painting as *pittura metafisica* ("metaphysical painting"), which can be defined *après* Weininger, as "an insight capable of elucidating the profound meaning of things."[6] In a phenomenological stroke, de Chirico resemiologizes everyday objects and spatializes the quotidian as manifestations of a metaphysical enigma: "we who understand the signs of the metaphysical alphabet know what joys and sorrows are hidden within a portico, the angle of a street or even a room, on the surface of a table between the sides of a box."[7] Indeed, the "eternal proof of the *senselessness* of the universe"[8] lies in the observation of the quotidian, in its phenomenological bracketing and its elevation on the observational plane of the Husserlian transcendental attitude. Remarkably, while de Chirico seemed never to have read Husserl, he nevertheless employs what can only be described as Husserl's phenomenological method to reach Nietzschean levels of reality.[9] This elective affinity has another facet too: de Chirico has been greatly influenced by the German romantic concept of *Stimmung*, namely "the momentary and reciprocal integration, which can create a fusion between a subject's state of mind and the atmosphere inherent in his immediate physical environment."[10] *Stimmung's* intentionality, in the precise Husserlian sense of connection between consciousness and external world (in Husserl, consciousness is always consciousness *of...*, and this is the only manner in which both sides of the equation can be materialised) relates deeply to the importance of the quotidian as an avenue of "looking inside." While intentionality is a useful way of conceptualising the interdependence of subject and object, it remains *enigmatic* in that its precise spatialization is perpetually elusive, fleetingly nesting in *entre-moments*. Precisely on account of this elusiveness, intentionality is one tangible way of approaching de Chirico's enigma: as the relentless oscillation between a psychological depiction of the world and a cerebral externalisation, paradigmatically pronounced textually.

Indeed, the charming discrepancy between the subtly suggestive nature of the landscapes and the occasionally inelegant descriptive titles given by de Chirico (e.g., "Enigma of the Oracle," "Nostalgia of the Infinite," "Anguish of Departure," "Purity of a Dream," and so on) points to a *conscious* effort of *abandonment* to "the dream reality" of the *pittura metafisica*. A luminous example would be de Chirico's series of Ariadne paintings, depicted as a statue in most of his piazza landscapes between 1912-

1913, after having been abandoned by her lover Theseus on the island of Naxos, and in anticipation of Dionysus who eventually comes to her rescue. In many respects, Ariadne is absent from these paintings. What remains of Ariadne is a passivity, a lassitude that laps on the melancholia of loneliness, without, however, ever reaching depths of depression or despair. Ariadne is asleep, statuesquely frozen in the middle of greenish piazzas, oneirically suspended between the departing sail of Theseus's boat and the arriving smoke of Dionysus's train, abandoned, exposed and silently mouthing one relentlessly repetitive phrase: "I want to be found." Nested between the folds of her ethereal body there is an invitation to the passage, in the form of stasis: "Ariadne's sleep is the moment in which abandonment and discovery touch, in which mortal and immortal, Apollonian and Dionysian worlds meet."[11] Ariadne, and through her de Chirico, unfold their languor in a *conscious* attempt to *abandonment*, or in an *abandoned* attempt to *consciousness*: neither of these states exclusively, but both present in a new in-between of suspension, creating the only conditions in which the enigma can reveal its trace: it is through the abandonment to the quotidian that the metaphysical enigma is adumbrated; but such abandonment is "conscious," vigilant, targeting the ultimate aim of the enigma, without however losing consciousness of the fact that the enigma can only be targeted when not confronted: only the invisibility of the enigma can be visibilized, and only through abandonment can the question be uttered.[12]

These tensions will be revisited below, while looking at the horizon. Before vision, however, there is a need for an aural visitation.[13] For Ariadne's sleep is solemn and silent, undisturbed either by the softest of breathing, or by the slightest of movement. Yet, there is movement and there is rustling. There is always rustling, but this rustling has been muted. Nearly always, not far from Ariadne's macabre cradle, a train is rustling by, traversing the background and underlining (by obstructing full view of) the horizon. In de Chirico's landscapes, trains erupt as if out of nowhere, always followed by large luminous clouds of smoke, always silently sliding by: "sometimes the trains speed by in the distance amid a silence which evokes an almost physical longing for the reassurance of their sound; sometimes they are animal-like and ferocious, as in the *Anxious Journey*."[14] In the latter painting (1913), there is no piazza. There is only a forest of superimposed arches oppressing the viewer and asphyxiating the landscape, with the seeming respite of an opening on the left side of the canvas, from where a train emerges, full frontal and fuming, hurling its crackling body onto a brick wall. But, instead of protecting the viewer, the wall encloses them even more in a labyrinthal *mise-en-abîme*, which, however, contains a promise, a soothing angst, an imperceptible, "pleasing anxiety" as Kierkegaard would say, reminiscent of the end of the train line on Mount Pelion—his father's masterful construction, which linked Volos—de Chirico's native city in Greece—with the mount of the centaurs looming above the city. Meliés, the end of the Pelion line, is simply a glade in the middle of the wilderness where trees lean down onto a solitary train station and create a piazza of silence and sweet anxiety, an amphitheatre of echo and exposed solitude, as if someone were watching. The train nowadays operates only twice a week, but in de Chirico's paintings, the paternal train departs and arrives continuously, the scent of a prodigal absence shaking on the horizon with its mnemonic embrace.[15]

Comparable anxiety in its ambiguity is produced in "The Surprise" (1914), where the landscape explodes with arches and mockeries of openings, leading invariably to more arches and more promised but invisible exits. The canvas becomes the landscape, the limits of the painting become the limits of the escape and de Chirico shows the viewer the enigma of the landscape without horizon. And then he plays with the viewer: in "The Enigma of Fatality" (1914), he implodes the chess-like landscape in the confines of a triangular canvas—a shape which, as de Chirico writes, "has served *ab antico* and still serves today in Theosophical doctrine as a mystic and magical symbol and certainly often awakes in a person who looks at it, whether he knows the tradition or not, a sense of uneasiness and almost fear";[16] or in "The Purity of a Dream" (1915), where the eruption comes from within: the landscape is contained within a frame at the back of the usual towers and arches, somewhat self-hanging and oddly delicate, depicting a thin and elegant tree in full spring guise. The landscape is given to the viewer in a package of simulacrum, all the more promising and disquieting for that, and the frame seems to be hanging from itself, not unlike some of de Chirico's later landscaped syntheses, where Roman villas seemed superimposed on incongruously lush and wild Hellenistic natural backdrops.

De Chirico's landscapes are fragmented, fissured, explosive, multiple, juxtaposed, unconnected. They are visual, but with a visuality that resists human vision and attempts a utopian plurality of regard which aspires to the eye (and the rest of the sensory organs) of the *über*observer. They are full of silences and muted eruptions, echoes of questioning phrases and screeching wheels. They are full of twilight odours, whiffs of Italian afternoons, smells of marble left in the sun, and dust in the subdued light of the sunset. They open up their surfaces to villiform skies, angular statues, rough arcade walls, soothing oriental winds and inviting boxes in the forefront on which to sit and ponder. The canvases perform the visual and utter the question; but at the same time, they perform the non-visual (and avoid the question) offering just a trail of the *au-delà*. The performativity and, simultaneously, non-performativity of the paintings are a resonance of de Chirico's Zarathustrian self-description: a constantly metamorphing god—philosopher—novelist—mythological personage—critic—surrealist—classicist—Italian—Greek—metaphysician—modernist; the celebrated source of surrealist inspiration and the notorious instigator of one of the most acrimonious catfights in the art world; the man who, along with Picasso, changed the art of the twentieth century, only to retreat to a sterile classicism capable of raising questions on whether "de Chirico has last his genius";[17] the personage who became the involuntary precursor of totalitarian aesthetics, and the prophet of the trans-avant-garde ahistoricity;[18] finally to become an Andy Warhol original himself, producing the same tested, tried, and tired paintings again and again and selling them for considerable amounts of money.[19]

De Chirico, as a painter and as an artistic personality, is characterised by a relentless replication, a monomania with the sheer act of repetition, a constant modification of parameters, an interchangeability of viewpoints, a juxtaposition of spatialities and temporalities: all of them, ways of escaping the canvas, pursuing an ever-receding horizon of questioning, and, ultimately, loving the enigma ("Et Quid Amabo Nisi Quod Aenigma Est?"[20]) that he never quite attempted to answer.

A quote from Ovid's myth of the Minotaur is subliminally relevant:
 ...Appearances
Were all confused; he led the eye astray
By a mazy multitude of winding ways,
 Just as Maeander plays among the meads
 Of Phrygia and in its puzzling flow
 Glides back and forth and meets itself and sees
 Its waters on their way and winds along...[21]

Of course, these are none else but the corridors of the Minotaur's labyrinth—Ariadne's half brother. De Chirico places Ariadne into the maze, where the eye is led astray and the walls have no-sense. Through his paintings, the demiurge "glides back and forth and meets himself" in a relentless repetition of metamorphosis and rebirth, every time a step closer to the enigma, every time a step further from the solution. But there is a thread, a line that shows the way: when Ariadne fell in love with Theseus, she helped him find his way out of the maze with a winding thread. De Chirico's thread leads not out of the maze but deeper into it. The line that shows the way does not lead out of the enigma, but deeper into the melancholy of Ariadne, into her abandonment to an ambiguously expectant and relinquishing anxiety: this line, which has placed her on the island of Naxos, is the one that thinly and contingently separates abandonment from desire, maze from island, ignorance from knowledge. This line is taken up by de Chirico and, in a magisterial move, is stretched as the line of the horizon, luminous limit of the twilight separating the visual from the *au-delà*, the nothing from the what?, the search for the "other reality" from the "other reality" itself, the ever elusive transcendentalism limiting and, at the same time, urging human anxiety further and further. It is to the horizon that this text turns to now.

The Horizon

The landscape escapes as soon as landed. A standpoint affording an overview is to be found only in a continuous stepping back, zooming out as it were, physically trespassing on instances of precarious blind spots, backstepping on steppes without eyes, until the point of total escape is reached, veritable landslide where the land has escaped from its observer, just as its observer escapes his observatory in the ultimate attempt to encompass the land, the total land, including the arena on which the eye rolls and the eye sees from.[22] The *über*observer, gluttonously desiring to swallow the whole landscape, cannot but dethrone himself from the divine point of no description—in other words, escape the very thing he tries to encompass by jumping out of the picture, because *otherwise he can never get the full picture*. The visuality of the recession is a necessary metaphor, which understands human vision as having a *sense*, that is *one* sense, a sense of *direction*, *one* direction and not the other. In a sense, there is always a part left out, the part below and behind the observer, from where the landscape is observed. The further back, the greater the landscape, the smaller the blind spot behind, the closer a human comes to the lap of god. The further back, the greater the landscape, the larger the blind spots behind and before, the louder the echo of the falling tower.

Even if one encompasses the tower, in all its magisterial redness complete with flags and turrets, even if one indeed climbs up the vertiginous arched stairway and looks at the empty piazza blanketed by the green sky, one will be stopped by the horizon. Just after the train, marginally hiding the sail of the departing ship, following the trace of a brick wall, low on the ground between the polis and whatever floats above, a line brings forth what lies beyond by hiding it: "The horizon is empty. The wall seems to mark the limits of the world; there is nothing behind it. The sense of boredom and infinite fear, the somewhat questioning feeling produced by the horizon's line permeate the whole picture…"[23] The horizon stops the observer from climbing up the tower, fills her with an anxiety of the ground and of its infinity, brings her crashing down on the fingers of the greatest metaphysical negation:[24] *nothing* fills the canvas, *nothing* floods the landscape with the urge to escape, to hide and collapse under one's own weight, an enigma pounded on the sky as the trauma of the horizon fills her mouth with blood. But the same blood that enters like a fist and spans the distance between teeth, is the one that keeps the mouth open, an open wound as well as an expanse of vomiting suffering. The horizon reveals as well as hides, brings forth the unknown unknowns (*contra* Rumsfeld), drags the observer onto the limits of escape, and weighs down on the ground with an oppressive but revelatory question mark. The horizon distinguishes between here and there, this and that, now and then, by invisibilizing the there/that/then, and by making this process of invisibilization visible. Because the horizon only appears at conditions of clear atmosphere, lucid light, bright skies; and by appearing then, amidst such a luminous geography where hubris flies about full of confidence, the horizon shutters our illusions of divinity and reveals the limits of the eye by inspiring fear and trembling, "a fear we experience in the face of total intellectual lucidity, when all answers are known."[25]

In its paradoxical ambiguity, the horizon is, before all, a line on the landscape, a limit to the escape and the beginning of the land of scapegoats and centaurs grazing aimlessly in pastures of ignorance. The line of the horizon spreads on the background like a somnambulist, a soft, dream-like embrace of ignorance and innocence caressing Ariadne's eyebrows and opening her up to somnolent whispers from "the other reality," the anticipation of the arrival, the knowledge of the departure, the fear of the landscape, the anxiety of the limit. For, as Kierkegaard says, anxiety "is a qualification of the dreaming spirit.… Awake, the difference between myself and my other is posited; sleeping, it is suspended; dreaming, it is an intimated nothing."[26] Kierkegaard's *nothing* is not the void—it is a populated emptiness, precisely because of its vacuity. It is the object of anxiety, the begetter of anxiety, the intentional object of the dreaming spirit searching for "her other." In the state of dreaming, in the phenomenology of *epoché*, anxiety is revealed to the spirit as the other side of the distinction, the part of the canvas that is perennially left out, however much one backsteps or proceeds towards the horizon. The nothingness beyond the horizon is the terrifying possibility of freedom, "freedom's actuality as the possibility of possibility."[27] Balancing on the line of the horizon, palpitating in the shadows of the low brick wall separating the visible from the *au-delà*, playing with the folds of the fluttering flags atop the tower, there is anxiety and freedom, there is actuality and possibility, there is the ever-prior invitation to a hospitality of death and rebirth, the "anxious possibility of being able."[28]

Kierkegaard laments that the age of making distinctions is past: "It has been vanquished by the system. In our day, whoever loves to make distinctions is regarded as an eccentric whose soul clings to something that has long since vanished."[29] Even if Søren's days were different to de Chirico's, there is no doubt that de Chirico was an eccentric in the Kierkegaardian sense. Perhaps not in the strict religious sense, but certainly in a religious *non*-sense, in the sense of the divine diaspora, in the pluriverse of godly veils and celestial echoes. De Chirico's painterly soul was always looking towards the horizon, drenched in the anxiety of the discovery and the melancholy of never really discovering anything. The horizon is nothing else but this very distinction, the beginning of the receding realisation of infinity: distinction is the first gesture in a universe thirsty for meaning. Draw a distinction, any distinction and "call it the first distinction,"[30] as Spencer Brown would have urged. The first distinction, separating the trauma of existence from the place from which existence is observed, is the gestural magic of the divine wand, or of any epistemological necessity of assuming an illusionary omnipotence. From there on, there can be life and study. But what about the other level? How can the certainty of *super*vision be avoided? How can certainty (and with it, infinite power, infinite knowledge, eternal enlightenment, supremacy, Übermensch and *super*vision) be shown to have limits?

By positing the horizon. The line on the background of the canvas keeps a balance between the large flat expanses in the front and the towering arches and chimneys at the back. The balance, however, is almost constantly tilted towards the horizon, the trauma on the canvas, a wound that could have been created by Lucio Fontana's knives. The long shadows, the train, the distorted perspective, the flags, the collapsing sky: all point to the moment of meeting, where knowledge of the forefront and ignorance of the beyond melt into one another. The foreground too is full of pointers and reminders of the ignorance of the beyond: scattered objects that look beyond, into a surrealist firmament; empty wagons inviting someone to walk through them and find oneself on the "other side"; checkerboard floor leading in small jumps to the back of the painting; and so on. In Nostalgia of the Infinite (1913-14), the horizon is underlined by an oddly bucolic mountain range, and then pulled vertiginously heavenwards, following the verticality of the looming tower, and beyond, amongst the sonorously flapping flags tracing a wind from *somewhere*. The liberation and breathing space of such an elevation is begotten and simultaneously conditioned by a box, abandoned on the very forefront of the canvas, a frayed perspective of elevation yet landing, the burden of actuality pointing to the expanse of possibility.

Thus, the horizon stands for infinity (in another typical Husserlian twist), cognitive omnipotence, the flight of possibility; but it also stands for limitation, impotence, the end of possibility. The great importance of the horizon is not so much that it can never be reached; rather, it can be found in the singular phenomenon that the further towards the horizon one goes, the larger expanse is swallowed up by one's steps, the larger the blind spot behind one's back. The overview can never be achieved by running towards the horizon—so, how about if one went backwards, started running away from the horizon, in a frenzied attempt to see more, to have more to embrace with *sense* and vision? De Chirico has talked about this backward sense too, the *sense of prehistory*, as he calls it, namely the echoing of the origin, the cerebral turning towards the past, which is met by the *sensation of foretelling*, "one of the strangest and deepest sensations that prehistory has left us."[31] It is not coincidental that the two things are interdigitated for de Chirico: both his paintings and writings are excellent examples of a spatiotemporal fusion. One way of conceptualising such fusion would be through the double sense of *before*: on one hand, what can be readily understood as *before*'s temporal dimension, which denotes that something has come "before" me and indicates temporal priority (has come before me in a generation, in a queue, in a bidding); and on the other, what is eminently viewed in its spatial dimension, which refers to something that stands "be-fore" me, that is ahead of me, in front of me, facing me, and to which I wish to arrive. Origin and destination, mother and desire, pathos and pothos: a uroborous[32] flow of mutual paradoxification, a fate of claustrophobia in the cogs of eternal return, a textuality spread in time and space, a "before" echoing *before* me and *being for me* both Eden and End.[33] This circularity of *a*topia and utopia leaves one running constantly between the two extremes. And, in essence, it makes no difference whether one runs forward or backwards, towards or away from the horizon, engulfing or avoiding infinity. The sense of prehistory, just as the sense of foretelling, "is like an eternal proof of the senselessness of the universe,"[34] and, if I may modify, "of the *non-sense* of the universe." Regardless, one carries on looking. Looking in *one* sense is, in a sense, drawing a distinction between the one looking and the thing looked at. Looking does not alleviate anxiety. If anything, it reinforces it: it allows for greater waves of possibility and ineffability to flood in one's vision, it lets *nothing* in and vomits the void on the face of the mirror, it throws everydayness into the ocean of question. The world is filled with uncanny, the horizon blocks the flight to certainty, the demiurge observes helplessly the canvas tearing itself apart, and anxiety swims in the softness of its contradictory entrails. Anxiety remains the companion in what de Chirico has famously described as "an immense museum of strangeness,"[35] namely, the corridors of this world, with all its side-doors, staircases and emergency exits leading necessarily to the same horizon. Anxiety takes us by the hand and builds around us walls of protection and horror, where horror vacui and claustrophobias are brought together in batting acrobatics of hunger.

The Window

There is a way of capturing a whiff of infinity. In "The Enigma of the Hour" (1911), one of his early paintings, de Chirico explores the theme of a window in the midground of the canvas, on the back wall of the centrally featuring building, which reveals a glimpse of the final background, namely the horizon in the form of a piece of sky. There are two windows on either side of the central arch of the building, holed in the back wall, in a perspective of seemingly classicist harmony. The windows are only partly visible, since the curves of the portico obstruct the upper part of the opening. Through what is left, a nebulous greenish sky can be discerned. The same motif returns forty years later in one of de Chirico's multiple revisitations of the Piazza d'Italia, complete with Ariadne and *Stimmung*. In "Piazza d'Italia – Malinconia" (c. 1950), a similarly semi-obstructed window appears on the back wall of the midground building, just underneath an arch, allowing a glimpse of an almost fluorescent green piece of sky.

The window contains one of the main features of art of any sort: that of surprise.[36] Surprise, in the form of revelation, was a constant pursuit in de Chirico's art, even—or especially—in the minute arrangements of everydayness: "The revelation of a work of art (painting or sculpture) can be born out of a sudden, when one least expects it, and also can be stimulated by the sight of something."[37] The surprising rejection of any other form of artwork aside, the passage makes clear the revelatory value of the quotidian sights—and a view through a window is the exact embodiment of such everydayness. A glimpse of the sky in a blackened wall, a framed chunk of soft greenish air, a painting within the painting: echoes of vistas from train journeys of the kind the young de Chirico and his family used to undertake frequently due to his father's profession. The landscape appears more melancholic, less accessible yet more present when framed. Its overwhelming, larger than life, *horizon*tal qualities are somewhat *contained* in a frame, for the landscape is now filtered through a conditioning (the frame) that positions the viewer in the picture. Frameless, the landscape is self-standing and, for that, more threatening; framed, it repositions itself with regard to the viewer: a frame is the point of entry for the observer, since it moderates the dimensions of the landscape, from an unmalleable expanse to a sort of window which can always be shut off or passed by. In short, *a frame reduces anxiety, by specifying (in a surprising and, on account of its limiting function, revelatory way) the boundaries of the horizon of knowledge*.

Of course there can be no question about containing the enigma. In spite of the fact that an enigma must be posited, indeed positioned amidst the quotidian and must find a nest in the recesses of a spiritual lassitude, an enigma opens up to the possibility of possibility and releases its conditions of hypothesis in a whirl of self-annihilation. Thus, the frame may operate as positioning, but never as containment for the enigma. On the contrary, the enigma is projected through the frame and onto the horizon as the knowledge of the question (more accurately: the knowledge of the existence of the question), eager to be baptised in the aether of ignorance. Thus Kierkegaard: "the whole actuality of knowledge projects itself in anxiety as the enormous nothing of ignorance."[38] In the limbs of anxiety, knowledge and ignorance conflate while tearing each other apart in multiple mutual projections. Anxiety is the frame of the mirror that makes each thing look as if standing on its head; an existential trampoline which constantly flips its players: knowledge—ignorance—knowledge—ignorance— ... On the firmament of ignorance, the potentiality of knowledge slides about, cutting the horizon into thick vanishing slices; and on the sandy expanse of knowledge, the actuality of ignorance fragments itself in myriads of perspectives and reverberates through the abandonment of the landscape. In between these two, clement guardian of the floodgates of the canvas, the frame of anxiety: a window through which perfumes of knowledge and ignorance circulate whenever one bothers to look at the horizon.

The window reveals because it hides. It reveals only a malleable chunk of ignorance, and as such, it is an invitation to the possibility of possibility, to freedom, and to the enigma *obligato* of such freedom. If it were to reveal more, anxiety would have been only paralysing. If it were to reveal less, anxiety would have been converted into fear, that is a targeted specificity, simple moments of contact with the lifeworld, a quotidian that has not escaped the quotidian. But anxiety is much more than fear: it is diffused and without origin, it circulates freely amongst the edifices of the quotidian, and only addresses one object: *nothing*. In the first distinction, in all its primordial arbitrariness, nothing is situated beyond the trauma of the horizon, together with ignorance and the possibility of knowledge. Kierkegaard would have said that nothing is situated outside the walls of Eden, where both ignorance and knowledge, innocence and guilt await: "When it is assumed that the prohibition awakens the desire, one acquires knowledge instead of ignorance, and in that case Adam must have had a knowledge of freedom, because the desire was to use it...The prohibition induces in him anxiety, for the prohibition awakens in him freedom's possibility. What passed by innocence as the nothing of anxiety has now entered into Adam, and here again it is a nothing -the anxious possibility of *being able*."[39] When Adam (and Eve - *pace* Søren) cross the walls of the garden, they succumb to the guilt of the love of anxiety, which pushes them out in the wilderness of death and knowledge; but at the same time, such crossing is never really guilty because its origin is nowhere to be found: "Adam does not know what it means to die."[40] There is no prior knowledge of the outside, just the urge of anxiety. In that sense, guilt is wrapped in a veil of innocence (and vice versa) large enough to *hide* everything but the possibility of possibility. The answer to the enigma will never be revealed ("there is nothing to explain, yet the enigma remains"[41]), and the enigma will remain always invisible, always beyond the collapsing horizon or hidden in the shady depths of blind spots. But something *will* become visible: the very invisibility of such enigma, the luminosity of the existence of the question, the splendid futility of the paradox will become framed in a window of visibility, just enough to reveal that it cannot reveal. But there were no windows on that "first" wall to afford a glimpse of the outside. Crossing from the garden into the "chessboard where the only pawn roaming free is death," as Cocteau once said about de Chirico's, was a blind fall into a never-framed horizon. Eden was an enclosure of asphyxiating knowledge about knowledge, and an agoraphobic lack of knowledge about ignorance. The wall had to be violated. But to encounter what? A passage from de Chirico's novel *Hebdomeros* takes a glimpse outside: "at such moments it happened sometimes that the wall at the back opened, and then there appeared spectacles which were sometimes frightening, sometimes sublime or delightful: a storm at sea with hideous gnomes grimacing and gesticulating in hostile fashion on the foaming crests of the waves, and sometimes also a springtime landscape, astonishing in its poetry and tranquillity: hills of delicate green framed a path with almond trees shading the edges."[42] So, would you have pulled down the wall? Or perhaps you may have just thrown the apple on the wall instead of biting it? But would a hole in the wall stop the "hideous gnomes" from flooding in the garden, while allowing the aroma of almond trees to linger in?

That would probably not be enough. One needs to have been exposed to the currents of ignorance, even in that uncontrollable awareness of a dream, in order to begin to understand the need to die. Prohibition is no longer enough. "If in the first light of dawn one can feel the shudder of death shot through with the shudder of eternity, receding into the beginning of time, then many a covering and many a veil falls before this feeling."[43] One needs to have fallen in order for anxiety to become urging, the horizon to become luminous, and the currents of the twilight to start circulating through the windows.

Notes

1. F. Nietzsche, *The Birth of Tragedy*, in *The Complete Works of Friedrich Nietzsche*, ed. Oscar Levy (London: Foulis, 1909), 66

2. M. Martin, "On de Chirico's Theatre," in W. Rubin (ed.), *De Chirico* (New York: The Museum of Modern Art, 1982).
3. E. Curtius, "Nietzsche's Aesthetics," *Formes*, no. 11, January 1931, 6
4. M. Taylor, "Between Modernism and Mythology: Giorgio de Chirico and the Ariadne Series," in M. Taylor (ed), *Giorgio de Chirico and the Myth of Ariadne* (Philadelphia: Philadelphia Museum of Art, 2002), 33.
5. G. Lista, *De Chirico*, London: Art Data, 1991, p. 75
6. Weininger, in G. Lista, *De Chirico*, 25
7. G. de Chirico, originally published in *Valori Plastici*, Rome, April-May, 1919, cited in H. Chipp (ed.) *Theories of Modern Art* (Berkeley: University of California Press, 1968), 451
8. G. de Chirico, "The Feeling of Prehistory," in J. T. Soby, *Giorgio de Chirico* (New York: Arno Press, Museum of Modern Art, 1966), 248.
9. For an analysis of Husserl's basic phenomenological method in relation to utopias, see A. Philippopoulos-Mihalopoulos, "Mapping Utopias: A Voyage to Placelessness," 2 *Law and Critique* 12, 135-157, 2001.
10. G. Lista, *De Chirico*, 29. *Stimmung* is a concept originally derived from Hegel, subsequently taken up and interpreted by Schopenhauer and Nietzsche, and said to be evoked by painters of German romanticism, such as Arnold Böcklin and Max Klinger, both of them fundamental influences of de Chirico.
11. M. Gale, "Rewinding Ariadne's Thread: De Chirico and Greece, Past and Present" in M. Taylor, *Giorgio de Chirico*, 56.
12. This is exactly the enigma in de Chirico's oeuvre, *contra* A. J. Tamburri's ("Aldo Palazzeschi and Giorgio de Chirico: Decentralized Antitraditional Aesthetics," in B. Allert (ed.), *Languages of Visuality* (Detroit: Wayne State University Press, 1996) assertion that there is no enigma but for the mismatch between title and image.
13. But *"No music"*! De Chirico's mistrust towards the metaphysical or indeed explicative potential of music is well documented; see J. T. Soby, *Giorgio de Chirico* (New York: Arno Press, Museum of Modern Art, 1966), 245.
14. J. T. Soby, *The Early Chirico* (New York: Arno Press, 1941), 29.
15. See also de Chirico's *The Prodigal Son* (1922), where it would seem that it is actually the father who is returning to the Great Metaphysician.
16. G. De Chirico, *Metaphysical Aesthetics*, cited in J. Taylor, *Giorgio de Chirico*, p. 452
17. M. Ernst, "Max Ernst on de Chirico," in J. Taylor, *Giorgio de Chirico*, 171*ff*.
18. G. Lista, "La Trans-Avant-Garde ou le Retour à l'Art," *Artstudio* 7, 1987-88.
19. An extraordinary anecdote involves de Chirico's response to Madame Eluard's request to buy "The Disquieting Muses," which was already sold: "…if you wish exact replicas of these two paintings, I make them for you for one thousand Italian lire each." Cited in S. Symmons (ed.), *Andy Warhol (After de Chirico)* (London: Waddington Galleries, 1998).
20. "For What Else Should I Love, If Not The Enigma?," as he writes underneath one of his first self-portraits in 1908.
21. Ovid, "The Minotaur," *Metamorphoses*, Book 8, 159-166, trans. A. D. Melville.
22. G. Bataille's *L'Histoire d'Oeil* reveals the intentionality of the *Stimmung*, especially in the scene where the protagonist looks at the eye of the toreador rolling on the sand of the arena.
23. G. De Chirico, "Max Klinger," *Il Convegno*, Milano, November 1920, p. 42.
24. "Why are there essents rather than nothing? That is the question." M. Heidegger, "The Fundamental Question of Metaphysics" in *An Introduction to Metaphysics*, trans. R. Manheim (New Haven, CT: Yale University Press, 1959), 1.
25. O. Weininger, "Des Fins Ultimes," *L'Âge d'Homme*, Lausanne, 1981, cited in G. Lista, *De Chirico* (London: Art Data, 1991), 27.
26. S. Kierkegaard, "The Concept of Anxiety," in H. Hong and E. Hong (eds.), *The Essential Kierkegaard* (Princeton, NJ: Princeton University Press, 2000), 139.
27. Ibid.
28. Ibid., 141.
29. Ibid., 138.
30. G Spencer Brown, *Laws of Form* (New York: Dutton, 1979), 3.
31. G. de Chirico, "The Feeling of Prehistory," in J. T. Soby, *Giorgio de Chirico* (New York: Arno Press, Museum of Modern Art, 1966), 248.

32. In the Jungian sense of the word, where the snake eats its tail. See A. Philippopoulos-Mihalopoulos, "Between Light and Darkness: *Earthsea* and the Name of Utopia," 8 *Contemporary Justice Review* 1, 45-57, 2005.
33. For an analysis of the ambiguity of the word in a slightly different but essentially comparable context, see A. Philippopoulos-Mihalopoulos, "Before: Identity, Gender, Human Rights," in *Feminist Legal Studies*, forthcoming 2006.
34. G. de Chirico, "The Feeling of Prehistory," in J. T. Soby, *Giorgio de Chirico* (New York: Arno Press, Museum of Modern Art, 1966), 248.
35. Ibid., 246.
36. See A. Philippopoulos-Mihalopoulos, "Beauty and the Beast: Art and Law in the Hall of Mirrors," 2 *Entertainment Law* 3, 1-34, 2004, where surprise in art is dealt with from the autopoietic point of view, as part of *form*, in the context of a self-portrait of Lucian Freud.
37. G. de Chirico, "Meditations of a Painter," cited in J. T. Soby, *Giorgio de Chirico*, 1966, 251.
38. Kierkegaard, "The Concept of Anxiety," 141.
39. Ibid.
40. Ibid.
41. G. de Chirico, cited in J. T. Soby, *Giorgio de Chirico*, 1966, 246.
42. G. de Chirico, *Hebdomeros*, trans. and introduced by M. Grosland (London: Peter Owen, 1992), 21.
43. G. de Chirico, cited in J. T. Soby, *Giorgio de Chirico*, 1966, 248.

The Use of the Landscape in Heidegger's Philosophy

Gabriel R. Ricci

The Topography of *Dasein*

Martin Heidegger regarded the impulse to demonstrate the reality of an external world a moot philosophical point. Arguments to establish the existence of consciousness were likewise discredited. To Heidegger, and the phenomenologists before him, the reciprocity of consciousness and world was a given. The task of philosophy, then, was to describe what is presented to consciousness. Heidegger's analysis of existence in *Being and Time* was the first indication that any description of consciousness must include a world. In a manner of speaking, Heidegger painted a picture of the habitat of consciousness. *Dasein*, Heidegger's peculiar rendering of human existence, is attached to an environment, an *Umwelt* as Heidegger called it. Moreover, that *Dasein* realizes its proximity to entities within this world through a disposition of concern and care dramatizes the inherent attachment with which consciousness is predisposed. Embodied in this way consciousness entails a spatial and historical determination. Heidegger's resolve was to demonstrate that this special form of spatialization was explicitly temporal.

The consequence of the contiguity of space and time culminated in what we can call a temporal ecology. In other words, the space within which *Dasein* dwells possesses a temporal depth such that any particular space will not be confined to a discrete location. How Heidegger pursued this confluence of space and time will be explored through some of the metaphors he assimilated from the landscape to which he was personally attached. Heidegger routinely acknowledged the movement along a path which he identified as philosophical questioning.

Though Heidegger was dedicated to the explication of a fundamental ontology, he also disclosed an ethical perspective with the dramatic consequences of an ecological conscience. Heidegger's later critique of technology reveals the obvious connections we can make between his existential analytic and certain facets of contemporary environmental ethics. In particular, the manner in which the temporal dwelling of *Dasein* is incarnated in the disposition and mood of Care has obvious parallels in ecofeminism.

Equally critical of the western rationalist tradition, with the primacy of the autonomous self and its universalizable ambitions, and the hegemony of technocracy, ecofeminism ought not ignore Heidegger's analysis of the fundamental way that human existence is circumscribed by care. Granted Heidegger undermined these connections with his allegiance to Nazism, which had its idiosyncratic sensitivity to the land, but Heidegger's conceptualization of Care has a literary legacy which reaches back to Goethe and even models from the antique world. This lineage can be traced through a critical footnote in *Being and Time* which refers us to Heidegger's reading of Konrad Burdach's essay *Faust und die Sorge* from 1923.

In 1942 of *Being and Time* Heidegger makes the most persuasive case for the fundamental way in which human existence is literally grounded in the earth. Though human existence will forever be accompanied by Care, *Dasein* will always be called *homo* since it is made out of *humus* (earth). While it can be argued that Heidegger presaged the significance of care in feminist philosophy, his fundamental ontology is inclusive of both genders; human existence per se is predisposed to care.

Linking Heidegger to the care which is integral to feminist philosophy is incidental to our main concern that his ontological investigation demands that spatiality be construed in terms of the temporal. Though Heidegger emphasizes the worldly grounding of *Dasein* with what he called the pre-ontological myth of Care, his articulation of the temporal structure identified with Care is the real philosophical subject of *Being and Time*. This overlapping of time and space was endemic to the intellectual imagination at the turn of the century and was promulgated through Einstein's correction of Newton's universe in which space and time had been construed as separate realms which entities could occupy. Einstein's theory of relativity mathematically established the continuity of space and time. And the phenomenology of time consciousness elucidated in Husserl's and Merleau-Ponty's work would find a special ecological interpretation in Heidegger's existential analytic. In particular, Husserl's postulation of a *Lebenswelt*, a kind of metaphysical biosphere, would receive an environmental articulation throughout Heidegger's work.

In positing that human existence (*Dasein*) takes space in rather than occupies space, Heidegger conjured up a vivid environment in which *Dasein* dwells. Neither Husserl nor Merleau-Ponty embellished their interpretation of time consciousness with such colorful metaphors from the landscape, though Merleau-Ponty was emphatic about the manner in which the body mediates our existence. This sensuous mediation of the world, typical of the phenomenological spirit in philosophy, received its fullest expression in Heidegger's turn to poetry. However, as early as *Being and Time* Heidegger offered a graphic view of the topography of Being in which the fundamental *topos* of *Dasein* is cast in terms of historicity or what Heidegger called the "temporalizing of temporality."

Heidegger's incorporation of the historical foundations of existence was informed by his immersion in neo-Kantianism which identified the historical parameters of cognition. Coupled with Husserl's analysis of temporal consciousness, this historical perspective would produce a penetrating investigation of the temporal depths of mind. This aspect of consciousness is conspicuously absent from currents in the cognitive sciences which are rooted as much in the computational model of mind as they are the constructivist approach. Reductionism, which pervades the contemporary discussion of mind and consciousness, is not compatible with the phenomenological rendering of consciousness, since it is predicated on the spatial construal of reality. Though Heidegger would express the temporal character of mind with metaphors from the landscape he traversed, they were intended to indicate the history which supports human existence; that is, the space in which humans dwell is contiguous with time.

In his own efforts at poetry in *Aus der Erfahrung des Denkens* Heidegger imagined that "poetry that thinks is in truth the topology of Being." Moreover, poetry familiarizes Being with the place (*Ortschaft*) where its essence resides.[1] The revelatory power of poetry, for Heidegger, was an articulation of the ontological privilege uncovered in his analysis of *Dasein*. As such, Heidegger's appeal to the redemptive powers of poetry is a reincarnation of his early ontological investigations. More to the point, this poetic turn indicated Heidegger's frustration with the technocratic idiom which had colonized philosophy. The technocratic impulse distances humanity from its origins and obscures the vital connections intended in Husserl's metaphysical environment of the *Lebenswelt*. Poetry is the essence of the embodied continuity of world and human existence which Heidegger recognized in Hölderlin. In a manner of speaking, poetry reveals the environment which accompanies *Dasein*.

What might be identified as the symbiotic relationship of Being and *Dasein* in Heidegger's work was repeatedly illustrated through his use of metaphors from the landscape he passed through. Though it is well known that Heidegger's work was informed by Brentano's and Husserl's conception of intentionality, wherein consciousness and world are co-relative, Heidegger would establish his independence through the philosophical assimilation of the land. Brentano and Husserl provided a temporal mechanics in their conceptualization of intentionality, but Heidegger aesthetically embellished the temporality of human existence with a richness of place which indicated a romantic attachment to his environment. This relation to the land expressed a spiritual kinship which Heidegger would inflate into a metaphysical environment. Heidegger first articulated the dynamic of intentionality in terms of the structure of Care (*Sorge*). In casting Care in terms of temporal horizons, Heidegger relied upon Goethe's character of Care from *Faust,* Part II. Goethe, at the end of Faust's life, established that Care forged the inseparability of existence and involvement in an environment. At the end of his life, though he is even blinded by (the character of) Care, Faust proceeds with a monumental engineering project. The interaction between Care and Faust proves that Care is contiguous with human existence. This is the fundamental idea which Heidegger relies on for his ontological interpretation of Care. The genesis of Heidegger's work is obscured in his use of idiosyncratic terminology, but his reliance on Goethe is reported, as I have noted, in a revealing footnote in *Being and Time*. Once this trail is followed, one becomes aware of the literary pedigree for Heidegger's concept of Care. Goethe had relied upon Virgil, and there are even earlier sources in Greek mythology. Heidegger includes a myth which explains the foundational relationship between human existence and Care to fortify what he calls the pre-ontological basis of his thought. In spite of the neologistic haze that permeates Heidegger's work there are clues to the origin of his thought and the rich imagery of place always brings it down to earth.

Heidegger's meditation on Van Gogh's painting of peasant shoes in "The Origin of the Work of Art" is a model for the way that Heidegger's reflection, even on unpretentious imagery, calls up an entire world.[2] What Heidegger first takes to be the utilitarian character of the shoes, their "equipmentality" which makes them so reliable, is progressively inflated to include the "silent call of the earth" which the wearer encounters in their routines in the field. If there is an essence to the shoes, and if art makes this essence available to us, it comes attached to a world and earth which is synonymous with the being of a peasant woman. The awareness which comes with an examination of a pair of shoes corresponds to the intentional context of consciousness which makes objects available for practical use. Heidegger inherited this view of consciousness from Husserl's descriptive phenomenology, and though consciousness was determined to be coeval with a vivid environment, Heidegger did not infer any prescriptive or normative consequences.

As in the case of Heidegger's reading of poetry, this fundamental but detached approach to the proximity of an abiding world denies the real source of human suffering. In the end, as John Caputo recapitulates in *Demythologizing Heidegger*, there is a displacement of real life that follows from Heidegger's tendency to purge all that is not originally Greek.[3] Nonetheless, from Heidegger's analytic of *Dasein*, in which he revived the Kantian intuition of time, to the recovery of the inception of Western thought that marks the turn to the phenomenological character of truth of being, one can survey the terrain that illuminates the topological compulsion of Heidegger's speculation. It is a philosophically functional landscape that is distinguishable from the heroic and romantic appeal to the paths through the Black Forest that Heidegger would use to excite nationalistic pride in his students.

The strongest sense of place in Heidegger is initiated with the anthropological reality that *Dasein* is constituted of a there, a putting in place which entails a peculiar detachment from the world. This dynamic entails not just a here with the awareness that it is inherently concerned with its environment.[4] This temporal region constitutes *Dasein*, and it makes possible the practical relations with entities that are distinguished from it: those that are present-at-hand, or ready-to-hand. *Dasein* belongs to this environment (BT, 145) and thus there is an inherent ecological involvement which provides the basis for a praxis, thought it is not articulated. Heidegger, in his pursuit of a fundamental ontology, glossed over this implication and rather, defined *Dasein's* relationship with things ready-to-hand in terms of giving them space (*Raum-geben*), as if to allow them to involuntarily reveal their nature. When Heidegger does make an effort to thematize how the circumspection of *Dasein* might be realized, he speaks of activities that are relevant to building a structure, (BT, 146) not to any moral impulse that may follow from concern with the (social) world.[5] However, the Being-in-the-world that is the basis for further determinations for *Dasein* provides the existential spatiality that will circumscribe others. *Dasein* is located within the range of others, not with a mere attitude of concern as with things ready-to-hand but with a solicitous caring that is reminiscent of the attention one might give to the less fortunate or those in need (*Fürsorge*) (BT, 157). Along with the circumspection (*Umsicht*) that guides concern, this solicitous posture is enabled by a *Rücksicht* (consideration) and *Nachsicht* (patient forbearance). Heidegger had difficulty analyzing the psychological condition of empathy, and, in the end, reduces Being-toward-the-Other as a mere duplication of the self (BT, 162). Heidegger did not take the opportunity, as did Levinas after him, to extrapolate the moral consequences of this position; instead he bolstered his argument with a rather technical analogue from Humboldt's language studies which revealed that some languages use personal pronouns to signify location (BT, 155). Though Heidegger's analysis is not psychologically compelling, it did illuminate the temporal environment of human existence. That is, the here that temporally grounds *Dasein* is also a there and a beyond, and they equally determine the locus of *Dasein*.[6] What Heidegger does make clear is the aesthetic underpinning of this structure of care since he refers to it in terms of sight (*Sicht*) and what it means to have something in view. This temporal projection generated by human existence being thrown produces an historical transcendence which forms the substrata of will and intention.

The Forest Clearing

The root metaphor of sight is enhanced by the most illustrative spatial metaphor which Heidegger used to characterize *Dasein*, the *Lichtung*, or forest clearing. Literally the *Lichtung* is accessed through a *Holzweg*, a woodcutter's trail. As a symbol of the alethic force of truth in his work, Heidegger was somewhat possessive of this image. He would take Rilke to task for his rendering of the "Open" in which animals had a more privileged status than humans.[7] Heidegger's expression refers to an environment that is equivalent to the natural disclosedness of *Dasein*, and was intended to revise the medieval idea of the *lumen naturale*. The light of reason, which had previously been rendered as an inner light that shines under the right conditions, was construed by Heidegger as a clearing that by virtue of having been cleared (by the woodcutter's axe) was self-illuminating. *Dasein*, that is, requires no extraneous source to have access to the light; *Dasein* is constituted of its there, and in turn becomes its disclosedness (BT, 171). This primordial disclosedness was intended to emphasize that the Being that is an issue for *Dasein* is its location in the there (BT, 171). The image of the *Lichtung* is the primordial unity of time and space which establishes the locality where Being itself presences.

The *Lichtung* would have numerous manifestations in Heidegger's work. In his later turn to poetry in which Hölderlin is featured as the prophetic voice within this locality, the *Lichtung* appears as the "worlding" of the world in which what Heidegger calls the Fourfold (*Geviert*) is activated. This occurrence is a mutual arising of the four points of the compass—earth and heaven, the gods and the mortals. As with the *Lichtung*, beings achieve a self-presencing that overcomes the assertive framing (*Gestell*) imposed by the technological will. Albert Hofstadter, with Heidegger's consent, translated *das Ereignis*, this later manifestation of the *Lichtung*, as the "disclosure of appropriation." This interpretation plays on the word *eignen* which connotes personal possession.[8] As the model for the poet in destitute times, when the gods have fled, Hölderlin cried out from his home in the abyss of a durationless now, and summoned the destiny of Being. Hölderlin, on Heidegger's analysis, was quartered in the *Ereignis* and was consequently attuned to the mutual disclosure of the Fourfold.

The Uncanny and the Temporal Horizon

Heidegger's analysis of Care is part of his larger critique of the traditional subject/object relationship. Customarily conceived in epistemological terms, Heidegger adjusted this relationship to reflect the emotional and historical grounding which is simultaneous with existence. Alfred North Whitehead did something similar in *Adventure in Ideas* when he adopted the Quaker term "concern" to express the emotional bond between the subject and object. Consequently, for Heidegger, understanding is always preceded by a mood, or the realization that one finds oneself in a certain state. The German verb *befinden*, which is used to ask how one is doing, was converted by Heidegger into the requisite predisposition for understanding something about the world. The use of this common expression connotes an orientation to a place.

The mood or state of mind which is most delineated in *Being and Time* is anxiety. Heidegger has transformed this common feeling into the primordial mood that attunes us to the appropriation of possibilities. The gravest anxiety comes in the face of being-toward-death which consequently brings all possibilities into view. Like the disposition of Care, this sort of anticipation provides a sense of totality. This state of mind, more than any other, discloses *Dasein* and is accompanied by another feeling that Heidegger conceives in terms of place.

The individuating tendency of authentic *Dasein* requires that one be wrenched from the commonplace. Heidegger likens the insecurity of this movement to being away from home, *unheimlich* (BT, 233). No change in the environment need bring on the occasion of anxiety; it is an original condition that frees *Dasein* for its ownmost potentiality for Being. Once again, Heidegger offers no prescription for the way that the anticipation of death can improve the quality of life; facing it as one's ownmost possibility merely frees us from the herd mentality of *das Man*, who is occupied with the quotidian and intent on fitting in. Nietzsche offers a more poignant interpretation of this mentality in his well-known description of slave and master morality. Heidegger's analysis raises the question of how being away from home, the place of familiarity, can coincide with this potentiality for Being.

One must look to the way that *Dasein* is really a structural whole to answer this question. If *Dasein* is comported toward a future potentiality, then it makes sense that *Dasein* is already beyond itself; its kind of being necessarily consists of what is possible. Heidegger formally describes this as a Being-ahead-of-itself, which is just one of the temporal facets of the care structure. Together with Being-in-the-world and Being-alongside-entities, this futural capacity rounds off the totality of *Dasein*. Care, then, is not a particular attitude that one merely takes up, it is an ontological predisposition that is evinced in anxiety.

Heidegger concedes the tendency to conceive of *Dasein's* situation of the "there" in spatial terms, but this concession comes with reservations (BT, 346). This is made clear in the way the attitude of resoluteness grounds the situation of being authentically comported towards potentiality-for-Being. At this juncture in *Being and Time* the temporalizing quality of *Dasein's* situation becomes clear; it is through anticipatory resoluteness that temporality is fundamentally exposed (BT, 351). The predisposition of totality arises from an ontical possibility of *Dasein*, that is, death, and comes with the awareness that the possibility of nullity has its basis in the care structure of *Dasein*.

Death is not something that is tacked on at the end (BT, 354). Ontologically conceived, anticipatory resolution in the face of death reveals that *Dasein* is composed of indefinite possibilities. Authentically directed toward the end is equivalent to what Heidegger provocatively calls "wanting to have a conscience" (BT, 357). Accordingly, *Dasein* does not flee from the world on this impulse, it is instead a directive to take some kind of action; still nothing in particular is prescribed (BT, 358). It is easy to see why some commentators believe that Heidegger does not successfully make the transition from the profound alienation of *Dasein*, in its anticipation in the face of death, to real activity within a social world. In this regard David Couzens Hoy reminds us that Heidegger only intended to explicate an ontological principle. However, Hoy does grant Heidegger the subjectivizing implications of anxiety since it provokes a concern for one's fate.[9] Moreover, we can not ignore the fact that Heidegger's use of Care in his analytic is suggestive of attending to someone or something. What Heidegger seems to suggest is what was at the heart of John Dewey's analysis of experience in *Reconstruction in Philosophy*, that experience is accompanied by the insight which directs it (experience) to its own improvement.

The resolute and consequently critical posture of *Dasein* stems from the futural projection that initiates the transcendent unity of the facets of time. Heidegger characterizes this movement as an ecstasy and distinguishes it from the ordinary sense of time which is construed as a sequence of nows (BT, 377). This primordial temporality is equivalent to the care structure of *Dasein* and confirms that the original spatiality of *Dasein* is a being within time, *die Innerzeitkeit* (BT, 382).

If the ecstasy that unifies *Dasein* means that authentic temporality does not devolve into a sequence of nows, then the past, present and future are really contemporaneous; temporality generates a totality within itself. This unity possesses what Heidegger calls a kind of horizon, providing yet another *topos* in the ontological environment to which *Dasein* is thrown (BT, 416). To each of the ecstatic points which encompass *Dasein* there is a *Wohin*, a to where, that makes up this historical design. Hans-Georg Gadamer would popularize this horizonal schematic in his exposition of the hermeneutic structure of existence, but this strategy had already been articulated in German historiography.[10] In each case the *Wohin* that defines the temporal modes amounts to a disclosure that sparks an attentiveness to an environment in which entities can be grasped and understood. This horizon is an inner effective-history that is the structure of temporally lived experience, not unlike Henri Bergson's internal duration in which there is a similar condensing of the facets of time. Indeed, before Heidegger's efforts to delineate the historical character of human existence, Bergson had already intuited the duration constitutive of human existence. In his challenge to a universal science derived from one principle, Bergson illuminated the internal duration which is not mere juxtaposition, but a succession which is a development from within and which constitutes an extension of the past into the present and which is already tied to the future. In imagining how the mind might intuitively reflect upon itself, Heidegger and Bergson required that we first begin with the way in which our kind of existence is temporally circumscribed. Their insights, I think, still present a problem to those who seek to delineate the mind in strictly spatial terms, as if it occupies a locus.

To accurately construe *Dasein*, Heidegger argued, we must first realize that any space that we may reserve to delimit *Dasein* is to simultaneously acknowledge the leeway (*Spielraum*) that extends into the future and reverberates with having-been (BT, 419). This special marriage of space and time is unique to Heidegger, but owes much to the conceptualization of effective-history in German historiography that can be traced to Heinrich von Sybel's theoretical manifesto in the first issue of *Hisotrische Zeitschrift* (1859) in which the Rankean dictum *wie es eigentlich gewesen* was challenged in favor of a more activist position oriented toward the future. Heidegger's peculiar adaptation of what the historian Eduard Meyer dubbed *historische Wirksame*, historical efficacy, is devoid of the political vigor that captured Ranke's early detractors, but vestiges of this assault on Ranke are present in the later sections of *Being and Time*.

In granting the leeway that has already been temporally defined, there is simultaneously generated what Heidegger calls a region in which there is a spontaneous rapport with practical activity. This leeway was first characterized as a simultaneous alignment or centering (*Ausrichtung*) and de-severance (*Ent-fernung*) which is to be understood as the capacity for *Dasein* to overcome remoteness or distance (BT, 138). *Dasein*, in other words, is disposed to bring things close. This capacity for involvement is grounded in the ability to manipulate space and distance in the manner that surveying the land with instruments overcomes actual distances by transforming them into graphic and mathematical notations. The assessment of *Dasein's* spatial range readily corresponds to the ability of making things present that derives from the primordial temporal unity which is embodied in the concept of Care (*Sorge*). With the temporal conversion of *Dasein's* manipulation of space we are cautioned not to view the "here" that is generated as occupying a space; rather, it is, according to Heidegger, only a leeway that has become activated through the process of bringing-into-alignment (*Ausrichtung*) and overcoming-distance (*Ent-fernung*). These concerns might very well occupy someone who is building a house and must consider sighting a structure, leveling a dwelling or joining timbers. It is no wonder that Heidegger has chosen to capture this temporal dwelling in the word care. Before he expressly concerned himself with the way that technocracy had distorted humanity's relationship with the world, Heidegger had already put into place a definitive ecological framework for *Dasein*.

Language and the Path of Silence

In his "Letter on Humanism," Heidegger resuscitated the ontological privilege of *Dasein* that traditional humanism had overlooked. This effort revived the fundamental ontology in *Being and Time* which distinguished *Dasein* as abiding within the clearing (*Lichtung*) of Being. Equally, the essay highlighted the salutary effects of poetry that Heidegger had been occupied with since the 1930s. Heidegger was chiefly concerned with two issues: the way that language had gone astray in the technological age, and how aping the sciences had kept philosophy from technical thinking.[11] The standard by which thinking ought to be judged requires that we liberate thinking from technical thinking that is designed for calculation and systematic labeling. If an adequate measure is to be found, then we are required to recover the sense of language that is not restricted to mere signifying, but which phenomenologically opens onto the world. To this analysis, Heidegger would erect yet another revelatory structure within which we dwell–language itself. This would be the kind of dwelling through which we are primordially at home. Ironically, the risk of discovery in this instance might mean that we might find that we have very little to say. Finding ourselves at home in the nearness of Being (*Lichtung*) requires that we become adjusted to the nameless,[12] the opposite mode of calculative language that is obsessed with classification and differentiation.

To identify the true worth of human existence, Heidegger relies on his exposition of the real substance of *Dasein* in *Being and Time*. The *Da* now denotes the *a priori* privilege through which the temporal ecstasy of *Dasein* engages the truth of Being. This configuration is designated as the movement of concealing-unconcealing that takes place in the *Lichtung*. This reading of care is represented in the imagery of a shepherd.[13] Cast in these terms, *Dasein* is bequeathed the responsibility for maintaining Being with the care that a shepherd would provide for his flock. Thus we are transported to a heather-covered knoll where the attentiveness of the shepherd on an outcropping supplants the technical idiom of the academic philosopher.

The metaphysical import of language is concealed when it is not interpreted in accord with Being. The essence of language is the house of Being and as such, Heidegger concludes, it is also the home of the human essence.[14] This imagery indicates that the essence of language is not simply another aptitude, but a place in which *Dasein* is at home. Heidegger finds an expression of the comfort of this original place in Hölderlin's poetry. Conceived in a general way, this homeland, of which Hölderlin spoke, was a comfort to those Germans facing death (in the war). They adopted an attitude that was different from the chauvinistic response typical of most Germans.[15] However, Heidegger might very well have given his detractors ammunition when he put down Goethe's cosmopolitanism in the same breath.[16] In the end, Heidegger urges us to go beyond representational thought which cannot adequately capture the peculiar "ek-sistence" of *Dasein*. Heidegger writes the word existence in this way to connote the ecstatic nature of temporal consciousness or the way in which we are mutually comprised of the facets of time and consequently always out of our place.

To enter into the place where *Dasein* stands in the nearness of Being, Heidegger recommends that we take a step back and enter into a questioning that actually experiences.[17] This rhetorical position implies a reciprocity between saying and (the experience of the) world which requires that we transcend mere apophantic or hermeneutic language use. This difficulty is overcome, Heidegger intimates, when we distance ourselves from the compulsive opining of philosophy and penetrate the obscured provinces of language through the path of silence.[18] This enigmatic advice is reminiscent of the clarification in the Kena Upanishad that Brahman is that which cannot be expressed in words but by which the tongue speaks. Silence (sigetics) can represent that which cannot be placed in words. These connections partially explain Heidegger's preoccupation with the thinking that occupies poetry and the meditative deliberation that is to be distinguished from the calculative thinking that is seated in volition.

What Heidegger meant by casting off the opinionated discourse of philosophy and entering into a questioning that experiences is illustrated in the *Conversation on a Country Path About Thinking*. The clever airing of views in this conversation claims the symbiotic relationship between saying and experiencing, but this analysis of the more essential forms of thinking also obscures the suffering and empathy that is the source of poetic thinking; thinking that Heidegger thought could break through the isolation of philosophical discourse. His preoccupation with maintaining the metaphysical backdrop of Being, it seems, insulated him from the genuine sources of poetic thinking. Veronique Foti's exposition of Heidegger's appropriation of the poets in *Heidegger and the Poets* uncovers this blind spot in Heidegger's work.[19]

Heidegger intended that this higher order of thinking is prior to thought. It does not demand technological intervention into reality, it seeks a composed and steady disposition that is reflected in the word *Gelassenheit* which appears in the essay's original title *Zur Erörterung der Gelassenheit*. The word connotes a detachment from the technological access to existence that would release us from a concern for the material ordering of reality, to a delivering over to the presence of Being. To be released onto the presence of Being means that the will is out of place, and so thinking abides in the original unity of language and reality that is obscured through the technical governance of reality.

The expression of homelessness that attracted Heidegger to Hölderlin's poetry is addressed along the path in reference to the calculative planning that reduces existence to automation and which colors reality with the quality of what Heidegger calls "standing-reserve" (*Bestand*). The loss of human existence's autochthony (*Bodenständigkeit*) is exile from the original steadfastness between heaven and earth. A kind of *axis mundi*, this position is precisely how Heidegger characterizes the mythic role of the poets in his analysis of Hölderlin's poetry. It was this kind of dwelling that was to provide the standard by which the originary soul of language could be measured.

The non-representational thinking and speaking along the path requires, as the term *Gelassenheit* suggests, a certain steadiness onto the region that overcomes the opposition between ourselves and an object that appears against an horizon. Intervention is inappropriate, since the word might also be rendered as "letting-be" or "letting-go" which suggests an equanimity and an acceptance that comes in the form of listening: the silence that "represents" that which makes representation possible.

Speaking and saying are not displaced, a naming in which the naming and the named mutually arise is realized.[20] The juncture at which the name and the namable detach occupies the space within which poetic dwelling becomes possible; it is only established in the constancy of the steadfast waiting which does not impose linguistic assignments, but which allows human existence to return to its origins in what is prior to thought. This configuration of the named and naming is a reiteration of the symbiosis of Being and *Dasein* and the self-disclosing capacity of the Fourfold.

Heidegger used the term *Inständigkeit* to refer to the release onto the metaphysical region that is the source of truth which would guarantee this spontaneity of thinking. This word implies a capacity for a constancy or permanence that would assure the endurance required to receive the nature of truth. Not piecemeal truths set apart from one another, but a reception of truth in its totality. This is all revealed in a poem that the scholar in the dialogue on the country path introduces to illuminate how human nature is released onto that which is prior to thought of the region of regions. That it is the "thinking heart" which is to be cultivated with a humble patience in order to receive the truth intact is a clear sign that belonging to this metaphysical region is not an unadulterated rational concern: *Nie ein Wahres allein./Bestell des denkende Herz/*

In die einfache Langmut/ Der Einzigen Grossmut/ Edlen Erinnerns.[21] Metaphysically speaking, belonging to this region also means that this region needs human nature, a reciprocity that is spelled out in temporal terms in *Being and Time*. To conceive of this region requires overcoming the tendency to objectify a relation between ourselves and the entity Heidegger referred to as *Gegend*, or *Gegnet* in its old form. As an open expanse, this incarnation of the *Lichtung* gathers everything unto itself in a restful lingering.[22] Nothing appears to happen in this region because things no longer stand opposite us. More importantly, nothing stands at all. [23]The state of *Inständigkeit* is an earnest non-willing that rules out, according to the scholar in the dialogue, ostentatious conceit, arrogance, and combativeness.

Moving along the country path was not an arbitrary metaphor for Heidegger; it resurrected the *topos* of the enchanting forest clearing through which the world is proffered in a movement of concealedness and unconcealednesss. The metaphysical region in *Gelassenheit* was also alluring territory. Its powers are not disclosed by linguistically mapping out the territory. Its secrets are revealed in the waiting which transcends representation. At once, this waiting is a deliverance from willing (designation) and a release onto openness. It is not a way (*Weg*) but a movement (*Bewegung*).[24] The unifying exchange that rests in the metaphysical region that we have access to through *Gelassenheit* and *Inständigkeit* is a reiteration of the totality which constitutes *Dasein* in *Being and Time*. In both cases, totality, or encountering the truth intact, is not gained through taking action, since action presupposes the manipulation of entities in an objectified field. The premise of an objectified field and an independent cognitive awareness, which conventionalizes the field through linguistic assignments and the consequent manipulation of the field, is to be contrasted with the primordial unity of the metaphysical region and releasement onto the region in that state Heidegger called *Inständigkeit*.

It makes sense, then, that Heidegger conceived of language not as an appendage of human existence that can be controlled like a tool, but as a region in which we reside. In respect to dwelling poetically, which is not restricted to poets, being inside language means that language (*qua* Being) uses us: it calls upon us to linguistically frame the range of what is expressible. Here, Heidegger draws our attention to the symbiotic relationship between human existence and Being. We come onto Being through the correspondence established in the poetic response which translates the movement onto truth into living words. This means, then, that this poetic response onto truth and Being establishes translation (transposition) as the paradigm for any further assessment of human existence. This root paradigm, however, does not entail translation from one language to another, but the transposition of the breadth of what is sayable into spontaneous thinking. Following Heidegger, there is no simple correspondence between the domain of what is sayable and naming, As the one domain does not extend into the other. Naming does not have jurisdiction over the range of the sayable, it is contiguous and primordially near-at-hand.

Poetically We Dwell

It is primarily in the poetry of Hölderlin that Heidegger sought the power to break through the conceit and self-exaltation of philosophy that had become mesmerized by its own technical idiom: an idiom that was fixed on entities and which had seemingly abandoned its original quest. Hölderlin's poetry would transport Heidegger to an originary *topos* that brings us full circle in his work. Besides being transported to the shores of the ancient Greek world where he sought solidarity for his Germanic roots, Heidegger was also transported to the mythical regions between the sky and the earth that recalls cosmogonic tales and the institution of humanity. In this region Heidegger evinces the Vichian postulate of the poetic posture of prototypical humanity. The primordial poetic wisdom with which Vico's "*Urmenschen*" overcame the "sacred terrors" of the forests and created *luci* (the Vichian analogue for Heidegger's forest clearing) meant that in the infancy of the human world men were sublime poets.[25]

In his essay *Erläuterungen zu Hölderlins Dichtung*, Heidegger took up the theme of poetic thinking when he examined Hölderlin's use of the phrase *dichterisch wohnet der Mensch* in the poem "In Lieblicher Blaue." The poem is a meditation on humanity's relationship to God. Hölderlin's reflection on the image of a steeple projecting into the blue heavens soon turns to the question of humanity's reach for the divine, and the real issue of the measure of humanity comes to the fore. The steeple is symbolic of the stretching (axis mundi) required to grasp the eternal. With Hölderlin raising the question of the criteria required for union with God, Heidegger uncovers the question of how humanity dwells. The measure that could guide us is as obvious as the sky for Hölderlin, but this standard is not to be gauged by anything humanity has merited or achieved. That humanity is replete with things it has acquired is secondary to how it is humanity dwells. The standard to measure humanity, according to Hölderlin, is captured in the idea that we dwell poetically.

The measure that gauges human existence, then, is not found on this earth (in the form of an object): "Giebt es auf Erden ein Masse? Es giebt keines," (Hölderlin, section II of "In Lieblicher Blaue"). This is precisely what we are to derive from Heidegger's dialogue on *Gelassenheit*, since the question of human nature involves understanding something that is, strictly speaking, not part of our kind of existence; but something that appropriates us. This puzzle directs the dialogue from its inception and is resolved in the same manner that Hölderlin measures human nature. Human nature derives its essence from the way it resides or is ontologically seated; in the same way that the interlocutors in Heidegger's dialogue discover that meditative thinking is not determined by thinking but through the metaphysical region that is revealed through a vigilant *Gelassenheit*. How human existence dwells first brings forth its nature; it is not determined by technological prowess. To construe the manner in which human existence is ontologially seated (dwells) is to marshal a criterion that is not used to calculate comparison, what we would expect with an emphasis on merits and accomplishments. Rilke's advice to the poet in *Letters to a Young Poet* is apropos: the poet must wait the creative hour with a deep humility and patience; to concern oneself with tallying achievements is a distraction. The poet must be as one looking onto eternity.[26]

The temporal in-between of *Dasein* in *Erläuterungen zu Hölderlins Dichtung* is cast in terms of the state of the poet who is thrown between the gods and humanity. In this state the poet summons cultural institutions and the civil world. Heidegger, quoting Hölderlin, indicates that poetry as "the most innocent of all enterprises" requires that the poet be thrown out from the usual fare of the day (*aus dem Gewöhnlichen des Tages*).

With his analysis of Hölderlin's poetry, Heidegger has assigned the obligation of rising above *das Man* to the poet as cultural mediator. Thrown into this place means that the poet must also transcend an artifactual link with the past, and enliven the future in the movement Heidegger identified as *Wiederholung* or repetition in *Being and Time*. Dwelling poetically and *Dasein,* it seems, are both heralds of history.

Echoing Vico's thesis of the primordial poetic apprehension of reality, Heidegger credits the poet with the founding of nations and the emergence of the historical, for he becomes active in the time that the gods have abandoned the world and the future gods have yet to appear. This was Heidegger's way of addressing the vacuousness of the technological age which had stripped humanity of its primordial ties to the earth. The poet, then, is in advance of history in this barren state and in response to divine signals envisions a future which is free from contemporary idols.[27] Composed of both a circumspective vision, facing both the past and the future in an in-between state, and comported toward a completion on the basis of initial signs, Heidegger's analysis of poetic dwelling brings us full circle to the analysis of *Dasein* inaugurated in *Being and Time*.

The mission of the poet, when thrown into the in-between, is to mediate the relationship between the signs of the gods and the "voice of the people" (Hölderlin's expression for the kind of tales in which a people are mindful of its relationship to the totality of beings, following his poem "Voice of the People"). This thrown state, denoted by Heidegger's use of the word ek-sistence (from *ekstasis*) means that the poet, like *Dasein*, is situated between the past as having-been and the future as anticipated completion. In this communicative and institutive role, situated between memory and anticipation, human existence, like the poet, is disclosed as instinctively productive.

From the vantage point of the *Augenblick*, the temporal in-between in *Being and Time,* the poet resolves what humanity is to become and how existence (*Dasein*) is to take up its abode.[28] The essence of poetry, which Heidegger locates in Hölderlin's work, is historical in the deepest sense, for it deals in advance with historical time. Poetry takes on the temporalizing of temporality which is the fundamental activity of the historicity of *Dasein*. This instituting of the historical world is not mediated by technical knowledge but by finding contentment in the extreme isolation of the in-between where, Hölderlin mused, the stout-hearted arise and bear the abundance of the divine. ("Bread and Wine") Released from self-assertive willing in this in-between place the poet cultivates the "thinking heart" and is released onto future completion. This truth, which can be realized after thinking resides in silence, ultimately manifests itself as a need. This dynamic is illuminated in the advice that Rilke gave to the young poet in a letter dated August 12, 1904. This advice, I think, is a description of the way that the poetic-historical structure, of which Heidegger and Hölderlin spoke, transforms our lives and the world.

Rilke helps us think Heidegger further: In counseling the poet on how to deal with the vicissitudes of life, Rilke explains the mysterious way in which destiny moves our lives. At difficult emotional times, Rilke advised, we stand perplexed and alienated because a trauma has distracted us from the familiar (we are, in other words, removed from the now). We stand in a moment of transition in which eve the sorrow which has entered our hearts is concealed from us. This new thing, however, does not disappear, it is merely hidden from us; and, though it appears that nothing has happened, we have been changed in the way that a house is changed when a guest arrives.[29]

Preserving the World

Heidegger's essay "*Bauen Wohnen Denken*" was originally a lecture from 1951; delivered in a colloquium devoted to the theme "Man and Space." In his customary way Heidegger begins with an etymological flourish which demonstrates the fundamental relationship between building and being (*bauen* is just a version of the word *bin* which is commonly used to express a state of being as in I am [*Ich bin*]). The manner in which humans are on the earth, then, is captured in the expression dwelling which is in turn responsible for constructing structures which accommodate dwelling. Dwelling is obviously regarded as having an *a priori* character if it makes the conceptualization and experience of dwellings possible in the first place.

As in similar meditations Heidegger tries to show how a thing (anything) must be more than a representation for thought or an object of production subject to our will, as in the case of the bridge to which Heidegger refers in this essay. (This tendency, alive since the writing of *Being and Time*, was Heidegger's manner of supplementing the phenomenological investigation of consciousness conceived as intentionality which he inherited from Husserl.) The common construction of a bridge, which we ordinarily view as an aid to traverse a river or ravine, really gathers in its environs in such a way that any analysis of the thing spontaneously spreads beyond the discrete entity in and of itself. The building of the bridge takes on the character of highlighting the banks on either side of the river, enunciating the sky above and magnifying the earth to which it is attached. The manner in which the bridge really exists means that it gathers up the Fourfold, the primordial compass in Heidegger's philosophical landscape. The character of dwelling and building, intrinsic to human existence, also means "to cherish and protect, to preserve and care for, specifically to till the soil, to cultivate the vine."[30] Heidegger was never far away from the existential analytic of *Dasein* in his later work; the use of the familiar structure of care and the resurrection of his analysis of death as being-toward-an-end in *Building Dwelling Thinking* are signs of this echo effect.

Heidegger's purpose in this revealing essay was to trace the meaning of building to its source in which everything that exists belongs. In doing so, he once again articulated the care structure which is synonymous with human existence. In his later thinking, to which this essay belongs, Heidegger was once again challenging the epistemological construal of the subject/object relationship. Our preoccupation with imposing ourselves onto a world is a vestige of this technological perception of the subject/object relationship. This worldview demands that humans occupy space or regard space as an inner experience in which consciousness is activated. Heidegger's analysis of human existence consistently asks that when we think of humanity (man) we are also expressing the gathering (together) of the world. In *Building Dwelling Thinking* Heidegger elucidates the ecological foundation of human existence for he equated dwelling with "saving the earth." There are no admonitions or proscriptions in regard to the environment, and Heidegger explicitly says that saving the earth has nothing to do with using the earth in any way. There is a fundamental ecological awareness in Heidegger's thought:

dwelling, which is synonymous with preserving the Fourfold, refers to the spontaneous acquaintance humans have with the earth. To take the earth under our care, the consequence of preserving the Fourfold according to Heidegger, means that staying on the earth does not make humans pilgrims, but curators of the sort that make cultivation and construction possible in the first place. The security that passes to the Fourfold derives from humanity's kind of dwelling which allows the Fourfold to accompany things, like the bridge. This is realized in the predisposition humanity has for staying with things, or in phenomenological terms, the tendency to allow things to present themselves independent of any mental or representational manipulation.

In this analysis Heidegger can be said to carry the torch for phenomenology, since he was intent on demonstrating how, through the process of "staying" a world or preserving a world, we allow a thing to be "free for its own presencing."[31] There are surely vestiges of Husserl's methodological dictum "zu den sachen selbst" in Heidegger's formula for saving things in the manner that they are free to make themselves present, but there is the unmistakable stamp of an ecological consciousness in Heidegger's emphasis that dwelling for humans means the sparing and preserving of the Fourfold which encompasses Heidegger's philosophical landscape.

The sighting and consequent construction of the bridge, in *Building Dwelling Thinking*, is a process in which a location is produced, location does not make the bridge possible. In turn the creation of a location produces space, *Raum*, whose original meaning is to clear or free for settlement, as Vico expressed with the idea of the *luci* and Heidegger embraced with his ontological interpretation of the *Lichtung*, as early as *Being and Time*.

What might be called Heidegger's expansive view of the self is once again illustrated in "Bauen Wohnen Denken." This interpretation of the self dovetails with the inflated conception of the ego which is attached to ecological thinking. What is identified as the environmental aesthetic is typical of say John Muir's and Henry David Thoreau's meditations on nature. This aesthetic is distinguished from an artifactual aesthetic which focuses on human creations which are discretely circumscribed. When Muir reports on negotiating a rockface he calls up a geological history that speaks to him at every foothold. This manner of being connected at once to a long history and an ever changing landscape is analogous to Heidegger's understanding that reference to man means to simultaneously name the Fourfold. Following his reasoning, if we were to conceive of an old bridge some distance away, the bridge would not just be present as a thought in our minds: our thinking actually reaches the bridge; from wherever we are, we are also at the bridge. Overcoming such a distance is made possible because our kind of existence is not restricted to representational thought in which an external objectified world is delineated by a subjectively-situated understanding. If our thinking transports us to a location beyond our immediate presence, then Heidegger must be suggesting that we have the ability to be in more than one place in the same instant, at least in the way that Muir imagined his intimacy with the geological history at every foothold along a mountain trek. Muir expressed an explicit ecological aesthetic, there is no mistaking his insight that every phenomenon we examine is attached to an ever expanding landscape, limited only by the bounds of our imagination. This interconnectedness of all things is expressed in Heidegger's assertion that even the most profound moment of introspection can not elude "our stay among things," that even in the depths of severe depression we can not abandon the unity of the Fourfold. [32]

The literal meaning of *Dasein,* that peculiar entity characterized by being there, receives another formulation in "Bauen Wohnen Denken." Almost thirty years after Heidegger's analysis that our kind of existence is characterized as "being there" he explains how our existence is nested in relations to locations and through these locations to spaces which in turn allow us to persist through distance and time. This permeability of consciousness and world presents an alternative to scientific calculation, which, through its ambition to mathematically measure the world, tends to obliterate the connections and relations that Heidegger disclosed in building. This building, which is synonymous with our kind of dwelling and our thinking, forms the parameters of existence which predisposes us to join spaces and thus incorporate a world. When Heidegger characterizes our kind of dwelling as saving the earth and preserving the Fourfold, we can not ignore the ecological tenor of his insights. The spontaneity with which our existence summons a world of concern cannot mean that we stand over and above an objectified world, but that we are perennially defined by attachments and relations, what Heidegger originally called being alongside and being with others in *Being and Time* and which we mediate through care, a vigilant temporal circumspection, and even a solicitous concern typical of the kind of nurturing and support provided for those who might be in need.

Notes

1. Martin Heidegger, *Aus der Erfahrung des Denkens,* (Pfullingen:Neske, 1954), p. 94. *Aber das denkende Dichten ist in der Wahrheit die Topologie des Seyns. Sie sagt diesem die Ortschaft seines Wesens.* Otto Pöggeler has explored the ramifications of Heidegger's poeticizing that "poetry that thinks is the Topology of Being." A third linguistic alternative beyond the traditional apophantic and the praxical-hermeneutic dispositions, that is, the sigetic, is examined. In Heidegger's work, the sigetic does not embrace the Gnostic silence that dismisses the *logos*; it is an "eloquent silence" that develops out of the *logos*. See "Heidegger's Topology of Being" in *On Heidegger and Language,* edited and translated by Joseph J. Kocklemans, (Evanston, IL: Northwestern University Press, 1972) p. 115, p. 146. Pöggeler muses that Heidegger has not followed the well-trodden path in his questioning; he is obviously more comfortable along the forest trails that abruptly end at an impasse, p. 128.
2. Martin Heidegger, *Poetry, Language, Thought,* "The Origin of the Work of Art," translated by Alfred Hofstadter (New York: Harper & Row, 1971). What Heidegger perceived as the "reliability" of a simple pair of shoes opens up to a world in which such shoes would merge with the furrowed field beneath the peasant's feet; a setting in which a harvest is in accord with winter's chill. See p. 34 and pp. 46–48 for Heidegger's meditation on how an artifact can summon up the world in its entirety; both in its delimitations and in its unity. Heidegger also demonstrates the manner in which truth happens in Van Gogh's painting. The way in which the equipment character of the shoes reveals how a world is intended exhibits the dynamic of concealedness/unconcealedness that is captured in the dialectic of the *Lichtung*. Heidegger's capricious interpretation may take in more than Van Gogh ever intended, but his carefree approach demonstrates that even a simple pair of shoes, in his mind, is framed by an entire world.
3. John D. Caputo, *Demythologizing Heidegger* (Bloomington: Indiana University Press, 1993), p. 160. This distortion of the plurality of poetry conceals the difference between life and death and ultimately "neutralizes murder itself," p. 164. Heidegger has been energetically critiqued for his misappropriation and misreading of the poets. See Veroniques Foti's study *Heidegger and the Poets,* (Humanities Press, 1992) for an analysis of the way that Heidegger "reconfigured" Hölderlin to coincide with the "destinal mandate" of Germanity. In chapter 17 of *Heidegger and Nazism,* (trans. Gabriel R. Ricci, [Philadelphia: Temple University Press, 1989]) Victor Farias claims that Heidegger's "transubstantiation" of Hölderlin was designed to absorb the ideology of National Socialism into the essence of the providential German nation. Heidegger may have comman-

deered his reading of the poets to satisfy his chauvinism, but his reading is also in the service of the histo-ontological analysis of human existence with which his thinking burst onto the scene. If Heidegger has taken us anywhere in his reading of the poets, it is back to where he started in *Being and Time*.

4. Martin Heidegger, *Being and Time*, trans. By Macquarrie & Robinson (New York, 1962), p. 142. Further references to *Being and Time* will be incorporated into the text.

5. When Heidegger outlined how it is that humans primordially dwell in the Fourfold (*Geviert*) in "Building Dwelling Thinking" (1954) he relies upon imagery of peasants constructing a log cabin in the Schwarzwald to illustrate how ordering a structure contributes to the "simple unity of the Fourfold," that is, how the basic character of *Dasein* abides in Being. From the corner where the child's bed is nestled in the room made for the "*Totenbaum*," the generations are prepared for their trip through time. See *Poetry, Language, Truth* translated by Alfred Hofstadter (New York, 1971), p. 160.

6. The moral neutrality of the philosophical discourse in *Being and Time*, some would argue, is the result of Heidegger's move from the confession of his birth. In his early years Heidegger successfully manipulated the resources of the Catholic Church, but his rejection from the Jesuit seminary remained a thorn in his side and may have eventually led to his final break and the distancing from Catholic friends and colleagues. See Hugo Ott's review of this period in Heidegger's life in *Martin Heidegger, A Political Life* trans. Allan Blunden, (London, 1993), Part II: "The Struggle with the Faith of My Birth," pp 44-129. Though an ethical treatise is conspicuously absent from Heidegger's corpus, there might very well be another explanation evidenced in his research. As early as his qualifying lecture for the University of Freiburg in 1915, Heidegger was occupied with generating an ontology from within the framework of time and history. His lecture "The Concept of Time in the Historical Sciences" relies upon Heinrich Rickert's insights on the nature of historical conceptualization and was partially inspired by a sentiment from Meister Eckhart: "Time is subject to change and diversity: eternity is single and undivided" (quoted from Ott, p. 86). The influence from Rickert and the maxim from Eckhart suggest that the praxis Heidegger is most comfortable with is the historian's craft, but the point of view to which he aspired was located somewhere between the transitory and the eternal. Can this mystical space generate a moral impulse as it seeks a quietude with the unchanging? *Dasein*, the paradigmatic historical entity that is comprised of a temporal unity, may very well be a source of the kind of temporal dissonance that we witness in Hegel's phase of unhappy consciousness in *The Phenomenology*. Heidegger's footing in the real world might have also been dislodged by his own contemplation, though Heidegger makes provisions for *Dasein* to acquire a view of totality through resolutely confronting its own finitude. .

7. Martin Heidegger, "What are Poets For?" in *Poetry, Language, Thought*, trans. Albert Hofstadter, (New York, 1971), p. 108. Rilke explains in a letter what he intends by the "Open" which appears prominently in his work. Heidegger believed that Rilke, because he did not take into account the "spatiality of the world's inner space," could not grasp the potency of the original time-space unity through which Being itself presences, p. 129. See Michael Haar's *The Song of the Earth*, trans Reginald Lilly (Bloomington: Indiana University Press, 1993) for a clarification of Heidegger's antipathy to Rilke's "reversal" of the hierarchy of humans and animals.

8. See *Poetry, Language, Thought*, p. xxi. Hofstadter connects *das Ereignis* with the revealing powers of the *Lichtung*. The Husserlian influence is evidenced in both metaphors. In each case there is an environment in which truth arises from the internal process of self-appropriation and self-presencing. Hofstadter traces *ereignen* to an earlier incarnation, *eraugen*, which means to place before the eyes. This is the basis on which Hofstsadter extracts the phenomenological interpretation of truth as self-showing that is captured in Husserl's dictum *zu dem Sachen selbst*. Moreover, this etymological revelation reinforces the aesthetic force of Heidegger's existential analytic.

9. David Couzens Hoy, "History, Historicity and Historiography in *Being and Time*" in *Heidegger and Modern Philosophy*, edited by Michael Murray (New Haven: Yale University Press, 1978), p. 340. Following Hoy, it is easy to recognize that Heidegger's explication of the temporalizing nature of *Dasein* clarifies a practical discipline in the real world. The efforts of historiography, that is, are facilitated through the historical constitution of *Dasein* that is equiprimordially comprised of the facets of time. In turn, the resoluteness of *Dasein* guides the critical apprehension of history which is constituted of real choices. We must at least concede that when Heidegger postulated the categorial significance of historicity, he intended, along with the stretching along of *Dasein*, that there was a concomitant capacity to fill up this continuity by way of selection and choice. As the paradigmatic historical entity, which enables historiography, it follows that there is a value-relatedness that underlies the connectedness of *Dasein*.

10. Ernst Troeltsch, *Der Historismus und seine Probleme* (Scientia Verlag Aalen, 1977). See especially p. 33 in which Troeltsch regards history not as an addition of moments but as an intuitive unity and amalgamation *Einheit und Verschmelzung*. Troeltsch's conception of historical totality is grounded in a form of causality which by virtue of an inner sense and memory, with both spatial and non-spatial qualities, the present and future are oriented to one another, p. 56. This fusion of the facets of time is given a thoroughly ontological interpretation in Heidegger, but it has its roots in the methodological advances of neo-Kantians like Rickert and Troeltsch.
11. Martin Heidegger, "Letter on Humanism," in *Basic Writings*, edited by David Farrell Krell (New York, 1977), p. 195. Heidegger offered an idiosyncratic reading of humanism which was critiqued by Ernesto Grassi, a former student of Heidegger's. In his later work Grassi would go on to compare Heidegger's idea of the *Lichtung* to Vico's *luci*, the burnt forest clearings in which humanity set the stage for civilization.
12. Ibid., p. 199.
13. Ibid., p. 210.
14. Ibid., p. 213.
15. Ibid., p. 219.
16. Heidegger might have taken the opportunity to quote the famous passage in *Faust* where, in a moment of linguistic chauvinism, Faust decides to translate John I:1 into his beloved German. Marx's notion of *Entfremdung* is cited by Heidegger as a worthy interpretation of the historical alienation that besets humanity, p. 219. It is distinguished from forms of internationalism that try to overcome the subjectivity of nationalism fro Marx tried to think the original essence of humanity that is not bound by subjectivity, but is defined as an aggregate of social relations.
17. "Letter on Humanism," p.222.
18. Ibid., p. 223. See Pöggeler's analysis of sigetics in "Heidegger's Topology of Being," especially ftn. 11 on page 115. Sigetics speaks to the logic required to ask for the truth of Being as evinced in "the questioning that experiences." The logic of sigetics, I believe, presupposes attitudinal adjustments that are revealed in Heidegger's essay *Zur Eröterung der Gelassenheit*. The locus for the "questioning that experiences" is the mood of *Gelassenheit* which is like accomplishing something through an expressive non-assertiveness.
19. Veronique Foti, *Heidegger and the Poets* (Humanities Press, 1992), p. 78. Foti's thesis concludes with Heidegger's inability to address the poetry of Paul Celan, who carried the torch for Hölderlin, Trakl, and Rilke all of whom appear prominently in Heidegger's work. For Foti and others this oversight was symptomatic of Heidegger's silence on the Holocaust. We have discussed the many places that Heidegger's philosophy has placed us, this is one place he unabashedly avoided.
20. Martin Heidegger, *Zur Eröterung der Gelassenheit* (Pfullingen: Neske, 1959), p. 46.
21. Ibid., p. 62.
22. Ibid., p. 64.
23. Ibid., p. 42.
24. Ibid., p. 47.
25. Giambattista Vico, *The New Science*, trans Thomas Bergin and Max Fisch (Ithaca, NY: Cornell University Press, 1986), p. 187. Prototypical consciousness was thoroughly poetic, as Vico argued, because poet in Greek refers to the creator. (NS, 376) On the strength of this poetic apprehension of reality, Vico argued that the *Logos* should be conceived as the deed. (NS, 401) The poetic character of *Logos* antedates its rational construal, since speech originated in the sublime gesture attributing senses and passions to physical bodies. (NS, 402) Vico's allegiance to the more ancient philosophical discipline of rhetoric is partially explained by his formulation of the primordial poetic disposition which produced poetic universals; which, through their ability to illuminate the topical, achieved the generic status of types in a more inventive way. Heidegger's philosophy is similarly inclined, and the topography of human existence in his work resurrects the *ars topica* of classical rhetoric.
26. Ranier Maria Rilke, *Letters to a Young Poet*, trans M. D. Herter Norton (New York: W.W. Norton and Co. 1962), p. 30.
27. Martin Heidegger, *Erläuterungen zu Hölderlins Dichtung*, trans. M.D. Herter Norton (New York: W.W. Norton and Co., 1962), p. 46.
28. Ibid., p. 47.
29. Rilke, pp. 44-45.
30. Martin Heidegger, *Poetry, Language, Thought*, Building Dwelling Thinking," trans Albert Hofstadter (New York: Harper & Row, 1971), p.147.
31. Ibid., p. 150.
32. Ibid., p. 157.

Contributors

Jame Schaefer is associate professor of science and religion at Marquette University.

David Martínez is assistant professor of American Indian studies at the University of Minnesota.

Andreas Philippopoulos-Mihalopoulos is reader in law at the University of Westminster.

Matt Willen is assistant professor of English at Elizabethtown College.

David L. Kenley is associate professor of history at Elizabethtown College.

David S. Brown is associate professor of history at Elizabethtown College.

Patricia Likos Ricci is associate professor of the history of art at Elizabethtown College.

Gabriel R. Ricci is associate professor of humanities and chair of the History Department at Elizabethtown College.